I0517798

FOOTBALL FUN FOR KIDS

INSPIRING HISTORY MEETS INTERACTIVE LEARNING

LM TAYLOR

CONTENTS

INTRODUCTION

I was eight years old the first time I held a football in my hands. It was a chilly Saturday morning, and my dad had taken me to the local park. There, he taught me how to throw a spiral. The ball felt strange at first, but I was determined. With each throw, I got better. My dad's encouragement and the thrill of the game sparked a passion in me that has never faded.

Football is more than just a sport; it has deep roots in American culture, tracing back to the late 1800s. While the basic rules are straightforward, the game itself is layered with complexity. And fun! It involves two teams competing to score points by advancing the ball into the opposing team's end zone. Yet, beyond the touchdowns and tactics, football embodies lessons in teamwork, perseverance, and courage.

Whether you want to understand the game's history, learn about its legendary players, or improve your own skills, this book has something for you. We'll explore the origins of football, significant milestones, and key historical events. You'll also get in-depth profiles of iconic players—both past and present—whose achievements and personal stories are truly amazing.

This book is intended for all kids and young adults who are passionate about football or eager to learn more. It's for anyone wanting to enhance their skills or simply gain a better understanding of the game. It is organized into several sections. The first part delves into the origins and history of football, tracing its evolution over the years. The second part features profiles of legendary players, showcasing what it takes to succeed in the sport. The third part explains the rules, different positions, and strategies ranging from basic to advanced, helping you grasp how the game is played. The fourth part offers quizzes, drills, and discussion prompts that make learning about football both interactive and enjoyable. Finally, we'll explore the culture surrounding football, including fan traditions, famous stadiums, and the sport's impact on society.

I encourage you to dive into this book and immerse yourself in the world of football. Try the quizzes and drills. Think about the discussion prompts. These interactive elements will make learning more fun! The adventure awaits.

———

CHAPTER 1
THE ORIGINS AND EVOLUTION OF FOOTBALL

hen I first learned about the origins of football, I was amazed at how much the sport has changed over time. It all began with a mix of different games played in Europe. These games were quite different from the football we know today. They involved a lot of kicking and running, similar to soccer and rugby. It's fascinating to see how these early games shaped what would become football.

THE BIRTH OF AMERICAN FOOTBALL

American football evolved from European sports, particularly rugby and soccer. Rugby contributed physical, rough elements like tackles and scrums, while soccer influenced the game's strategy and kicking. The first recorded game of American football was played between Rutgers and Princeton on November 6, 1869. This early version resembled soccer more than modern football, with players advancing the ball by kicking it. Rutgers won the game 6-4, marking the start of a new sport.

In its early days, football was chaotic and dangerous. Players had no protective gear, and rules were simple. Over time, Walter Camp, often called the "Father of American Football," introduced key innovations, including the line of scrimmage and the system of downs, which added structure and strategy. Camp also reduced team sizes from fifteen to eleven players, making the game faster and more organized.

As the game evolved, so did the rules. One of the most important changes was the forward pass, which made the game more dynamic and opened new strategies for advancing the ball. Standardizing field sizes and scoring methods further helped shape football into a structured sport. Early football, particularly in colleges, was brutal and often led to serious injuries. One famous story from early football involves a game between Harvard and Yale in 1894. The game was so violent that it became known as the "Hampden Park Blood Bath." Players suffered serious injuries, and the game had to be stopped several times. This led to calls for reform, and even President Theodore Roosevelt stepped in to urge safer rules.

College teams played a significant role in popularizing the sport. Schools like Yale, Harvard, and Princeton had strong football programs. These games drew large crowds and generated a lot of excitement. College football became a big part of American culture, with traditions and rivalries that continue to this day.

As football evolved, it became less violent and more strategic, laying the foundation for the modern game. The sport has grown and changed, but its roots remain an important part of its history. As you learn more about football, you'll see that its history is filled with fascinating stories and important milestones.

KEY MILESTONES IN FOOTBALL HISTORY

Football's history is marked by pivotal moments that shaped the game into what it is today. One of the most significant was the creation of the American Professional Football Association in 1920, which became the NFL in 1922. Another major event was the NFL-AFL merger in 1970, which combined the best teams from both leagues and led to the creation of the Super Bowl, now one of the most-watched events in the world.

Technological advancements have played a crucial role in football's evolution. The introduction of instant replay has improved the accuracy of officiating, while advancements in protective gear have made the game safer. These innovations have enhanced the game for both players and fans.

Football has had a profound influence on American culture. It has become a central part of American holidays like Thanksgiving. Many families gather to watch football games together, making it a cherished tradition. Football also plays a significant role in community identity and pride. Local high school and college teams often serve as a source of pride for communities, bringing people together to support their teams. The sport has the power to unite people, creating a sense of belonging and shared purpose.

One of the most memorable games in football history is the 1958 NFL Championship, often referred to as "The

Greatest Game Ever Played." This game took place between the Baltimore Colts and the New York Giants. The game was tied at the end of regulation time, leading to the first sudden-death overtime in NFL history. The Colts won the game with a touchdown by Alan Ameche, solidifying the match as a classic. This game helped increase the popularity of football and showcased the excitement and drama the sport can offer.

The first Super Bowl in 1967 was another monumental moment. Played between the Green Bay Packers and the Kansas City Chiefs, it marked the beginning of a new era in professional football. The Packers, led by legendary coach Vince Lombardi, won the game 35-10. The Super Bowl has since become a cultural phenomenon, with millions of people tuning in to watch each year. It is not just a game but an event that includes elaborate halftime shows and iconic commercials.

Football has long been a symbol of American grit, hard work, and perseverance, inspiring athletes to overcome obstacles. The sport teaches valuable lessons about teamwork, perseverance, and leadership. Many players come from humble beginnings and achieve greatness through hard work and dedication. Their stories inspire fans and young athletes to pursue their dreams, no matter the obstacles.

The integration of football teams also played a significant role in American history. The inclusion of African American players in the NFL helped break down racial barriers and promote equality with pioneers like and Kenny Washington paving the way for future athletes.

As football continued to grow, so did its influence on entertainment and media. The sport became a staple on television, with networks broadcasting games to millions of viewers. The excitement of live games, combined with expert analysis and commentary, made football a favorite pastime for many Americans. The rise of fantasy football leagues added another layer of engagement, allowing fans to create their own teams and compete with friends.

In recent years, football has embraced new technologies to enhance the fan experience. Stadiums are now equipped with high-definition screens, interactive apps, and instant replays, making the game more engaging for spectators. Social media platforms allow fans to connect with their favorite players and teams, sharing their passion for the sport with a global audience.

Technological advancements have also revolutionized training and preparation for players. Teams use video analysis software to study opponents' strategies and improve their own performance. Wearable technology tracks players' physical conditions, helping them stay in peak shape. These innovations have elevated the level of play and contributed to the overall growth of the sport.

The story of football is one of constant evolution and adaptation. From its humble beginnings to its current status as America's favorite sport, football has undergone significant changes. Each milestone, technological advancement, and cultural impact has contributed to the game's rich history. As we look to the future, football will continue to inspire and unite people, creating new memories and moments that will be cherished for generations to come.

THE FOUNDING OF THE NFL

The formation of the National Football League (NFL) was a pivotal moment in the history of football. It all began in 1920 when a group of team owners met in Canton, Ohio. They gathered in a car dealership owned by Ralph Hay. At that time, football teams were struggling. They faced issues like high player salaries and the movement of players from one team to another. The owners decided that a formal league could help solve these problems. They called their new league the American Professional Football Association (APFA). Jim Thorpe, a famous athlete, was elected as the first president. This group included teams like the Akron Pros, Canton Bulldogs, and Dayton Triangles. Later, in 1922, the league changed its name to the National Football League (NFL). This marked the start of what would become the most popular sports league in the United States.

Key founders like George Halas played a crucial role in the early days of the NFL. George Halas, who owned the Decatur Staleys, later renamed the Chicago Bears, was a driving force behind the league's formation. He believed that a structured league would bring stability to the sport. Halas was not just an owner; he was also a player and coach. His dedication to football was unmatched. Alongside him was Jim Thorpe, a multi-sport athlete who brought credibility to the new league. Thorpe's involvement attracted attention and helped legitimize the NFL. These founders worked tirelessly to establish rules and organize the league. Their efforts laid the foundation for the NFL's future success.

The NFL faced many challenges in its early years. Financial difficulties were a constant struggle. Teams often lacked the funds to pay players and maintain operations. Competition with other leagues also posed a threat. The NFL had to prove itself as the premier football league. One of the first significant successes was the NFL Championship game in 1933. This game brought attention and legitimacy to the league. It showcased the talent and excitement of professional football. Despite these successes, the NFL still faced many hurdles. Teams came and went, and the league had to constantly adapt to survive.

Over the years, the NFL underwent several key organizational changes. One major change was the introduction of the draft system in 1936. The draft allowed teams to select new players in an organized manner. This system ensured that all teams had a fair chance to acquire top talent. It also helped maintain competitive balance within the league. Another significant change was the expansion and realignment of teams. As football grew in popularity, new teams joined the league. The NFL expanded to include more cities and regions. This expansion brought the game to a wider audience and increased its fan base. Realignment ensured that teams were grouped in a way that made sense geographically and competitively.

The NFL's growth in popularity can be attributed to several factors. One of the most significant was the impact of television broadcasts. In the 1950s, television brought football into the living rooms of millions of Americans. Televised games allowed fans to follow their favorite teams and players from home. This exposure helped the NFL reach a broader audience. Iconic players and teams also played a crucial role in popularizing the sport. Figures like Johnny Unitas, Bart Starr, and Joe Namath became household names. Their talent and charisma drew fans to the game. Teams like the Green Bay Packers and Dallas Cowboys built strong legacies that attracted loyal fan bases.

Television broadcasts not only increased the NFL's visibility but also changed the way fans experienced the game. Instant replays allowed viewers to see key plays multiple times. Expert commentators provided insights and analysis. These elements made watching football more engaging and entertaining. The Super Bowl, first played in 1967, became a cultural phenomenon. It combined the excitement of the game with elaborate halftime shows and commercials. The Super Bowl quickly became one of the most-watched events on television. It showcased the best of professional football and brought together fans from all walks of life.

As the NFL grew, so did its influence on American culture. Football became more than just a sport; it became a symbol of American values like hard work, determination, and teamwork. The league's popularity fostered a sense of community among fans. Local teams became sources of pride for their cities. Fans would gather to watch games, creating a shared experience that united them. The NFL also influenced fashion, music, and entertainment. Jerseys, hats, and other merchandise became popular. Football themes appeared in movies, TV shows, and songs. The NFL's impact on culture extended beyond the field and into everyday life.

The NFL's success can also be credited to its ability to adapt and innovate. The league continuously made changes to improve the game and the fan experience. Rule changes ensured player safety and fair play. Technological advancements like instant replay and advanced statistics enhanced the game's integrity. The NFL also embraced digital media and social platforms. This allowed fans to engage with the league and their favorite teams in new ways. The NFL's commitment to growth and improvement helped solidify its place as America's favorite sport.

The NFL's journey from a small group of struggling teams to a dominant sports league is a testament to the vision and dedication of its founders. Their efforts laid the groundwork for a league that would capture the hearts of millions. The NFL's growth and success reflect the enduring appeal of football. The league's ability to adapt and innovate ensured its continued relevance and popularity. The NFL's story is one of perseverance, innovation, and passion for the game.

THE RISE OF COLLEGE FOOTBALL

The role of colleges in the development of football cannot be overstated. Colleges were among the first to adopt and adapt football, making it a central part of their athletic programs. The early adoption of football by colleges laid the groundwork for the sport's growth across the country. The first intercollegiate football game took place in 1869 between Rutgers and Princeton. This game marked the beginning of a new era, where football became a key feature of college sports. Colleges saw the potential of football to bring students together and promote school spirit. It quickly became a popular activity, drawing large crowds and fostering a sense of community.

Key college football programs have played a significant role in shaping the sport. Schools like Notre Dame, the University of Alabama, Michigan, USC, Ohio State University, the University of Oklahoma, and the University of Texas have become powerhouses in college football. These programs have produced many of the game's greatest players and have set high standards for excellence. Notre Dame, with its rich history and storied rivalries, has been a dominant force in college football. The University of Alabama, under coaches like Bear Bryant and Nick Saban, has achieved unparalleled success, winning numerous national championships. Michigan, known for its iconic stadium and passionate fan base, has also made significant contributions to the sport. USC, with its strong tradition of producing NFL talent, has been a key player in the development of football. Ohio State University, the University of Oklahoma, and the University of Texas have all produced legendary teams and players, further solidifying the importance of college football in the sport's history.

Legendary coaches have also left an indelible mark on college football. Knute Rockne of Notre Dame is one of the most famous coaches in the sport's history. His innovative strategies and motivational skills led Notre Dame to multiple national championships. Bear Bryant, who coached at Alabama, is another iconic figure. Known for his tough coaching style and ability to build winning teams, Bryant led Alabama to six national championships. Nick Saban, the current head coach at Alabama, has continued this legacy of success, winning multiple national titles and becoming one of the most respected coaches in the game. These coaches, along with others, have helped shape the strategies and culture of college football.

The rules of college football have evolved significantly over time. While the basic principles remain the same, there are notable differences between college and professional football rules. For instance, in college football, a player is considered down when any part of their body other than their hands or feet touches the ground, regardless of whether they are touched by an opponent. In professional football, a player must be touched by an opponent to be considered down. Additionally, the clock management and overtime rules differ between the two levels. The introduction of the Bowl Championship Series (BCS) in 1998 was a major milestone in college football. The BCS aimed to determine the national champion through a series of bowl games, using a combination of polls and computer rankings. In 2014, the College Football Playoff (CFP) replaced the BCS, introducing a four-team playoff system to determine the national champion. These changes have brought more excitement and clarity to the process of crowning a national champion in college football.

College football has become a significant part of American culture and society. The tradition of college football rivalries adds excitement and intensity to the sport. Games like the Iron Bowl between Alabama and Auburn or the Michigan-Ohio State rivalry draw massive crowds and generate widespread interest. These rivalries are more than just games; they are events that bring together students, alumni, and fans, creating a sense of community and shared identity. Bowl games are another important tradition in college football. These postseason games, often played at neutral sites, provide a festive atmosphere and offer teams a chance to showcase their talent on a national stage. The Rose Bowl, Sugar Bowl, and Orange Bowl are some of the most famous and prestigious bowl games in college football.

The impact of college football extends beyond the field. The sport has a significant economic impact on local economies. On game days, college towns come alive with fans filling hotels, restaurants, and stores. The influx of visitors provides a boost to local businesses and contributes to the overall economy. College football also plays a role in shaping the identity and pride of communities. For many students and alumni, supporting their college football team is a source of pride and a way to stay connected to their school. The sport fosters a sense of belonging and creates lasting memories for those involved.

College football has also played a role in promoting social change. The integration of college football teams in the 1960s and 1970s helped break down racial barriers and promote equality. African American players who excelled on the field challenged stereotypes and opened doors for future generations. The sport has provided a platform for athletes to advocate for social justice and equality, further highlighting its cultural significance.

In the end, college football's rich history and cultural impact make it a vital part of the sport's overall story. The contributions of colleges, key programs, legendary coaches, and the evolution of rules have all played a role in shaping football into the beloved sport it is today. College football continues to inspire, unite, and entertain millions of fans across the country, leaving a lasting legacy for future generations.

———

CHAPTER 2
LEGENDARY PLAYERS AND THEIR STORIES

very time I read about these players and their stories, I get goose bumps! While there are too many great players to include them all in this book, read on to hear about some of the greatest icons in the sport.

JIM THORPE: THE MULTI-SPORT SUPERSTAR

Jim Thorpe was born in 1887 in what is now Oklahoma. He grew up in the Sac and Fox Nation, where he learned to love sports. Jim's childhood was filled with running, jumping, and playing different games. He was good at everything he tried. When he attended the Carlisle Indian Industrial School in Pennsylvania, his athletic talents really shone. Jim played football, but he also excelled in track and field, basketball, and even ballroom dancing. His coaches and teammates were amazed by his abilities. He seemed to be able to do anything.

In college, Jim became a two-time All-American in football. This meant he was one of the best players in the country. He was strong, fast, and could outplay almost anyone. Football was just one part of his incredible athletic career. In 1912, Jim competed in the Olympics in Stockholm. He won gold medals in both the pentathlon and decathlon, setting a world record in the decathlon. People were in awe of his skills. However, his Olympic medals were taken away in 1913 because he had played minor league baseball. It wasn't until 2022 that his medals were finally restored.

Jim's football career continued to flourish after college. He played for several teams and became one of the NFL's first stars. His versatility on the field was unmatched. He could run, pass, and kick with ease. Jim's talent helped him become the league's first president. He played a crucial role in the early years of professional football, helping to shape the game we know today. Off the field, Jim acted in movies and advocated for Native American rights. He wanted to ensure that Native Americans were portrayed accurately in films and had better opportunities in life.

Jim Thorpe's legacy as a multi-sport superstar remains unmatched. His achievements in football, track and field, and other sports have inspired countless athletes. Jim's story is a testament to hard work, versatility, and the ability to overcome obstacles. His dedication to improving the lives of others has left a lasting impact on both sports and society.

THE TRAILBLAZING CAREER OF JIM BROWN

Born in 1936, Jim Brown grew up in St. Simons, Georgia, and he was a natural athlete. He excelled in multiple sports, including football, basketball, and lacrosse, at Syracuse University. Jim's athleticism was unmatched. On the football field, he was a force to be reckoned with. He could run past defenders with ease. In basketball, he was just as impressive.

Jim's skills in lacrosse were also outstanding. His ability to dominate in different sports made him a standout athlete.

Jim's NFL career with the Cleveland Browns was legendary. He led the NFL in rushing yards eight times during his career in the NFL from 1957 to 1965. His powerful running style made him unstoppable. Jim won the NFL MVP award three times, showcasing his excellence on the field. When he retired, he held the record for the most rushing yards in NFL history at the time at 12,312 yards. His career was filled with incredible performances and unforgettable moments. Jim's dominance on the field set new standards for running backs.

Off the field, Jim was a strong advocate for civil rights and social justice. He used his platform to speak out against inequality. Jim founded the Amer-I-Can program to help inner-city youth. This program aimed to provide young people with the tools they need to succeed. Jim's work off the field had a significant impact on many lives. He showed that athletes could use their influence to bring about positive change.

Jim's legacy in football and society is profound. He was inducted into the Pro Football Hall of Fame in 1971, recognizing his contributions to the sport. Jim continues to be a cultural icon, inspiring future generations of athletes. His story is a testament to the power of talent, hard work, and dedication. Jim's influence extends beyond football, making him a true trailblazer in every sense.

THE JOURNEY OF WALTER PAYTON

Imagine a young boy running through the fields of Columbia, Mississippi. That boy was Walter Payton. Growing up, Walter loved playing outside with his friends. They would spend hours running and playing games. Walter's love for football started here. He joined the football team at Columbia High School. He wasn't just good; he was amazing. He could run fast, dodge tackles, and score touchdowns. Everyone knew he was special. His talent and hard work paid off when he got a chance to play college football at Jackson State University.

At Jackson State, Walter became even more incredible. He set records and wowed everyone with his skills. He earned the nickname "Sweetness" because of his smooth running style. Walter scored a lot of points and became one of the best players in college football. His performances caught the attention of the NFL. The Chicago Bears drafted him in 1975. Walter's dream of playing professional football had come true. He was ready to show the world what he could do.

Walter's career with the Chicago Bears was nothing short of legendary. He broke records and achieved milestones that many thought were impossible. One of his biggest accomplishments was breaking Jim Brown's all-time rushing record. Walter ran for a total of 16,726 yards in his career. He also helped the Bears win Super Bowl XX in 1985. Walter's hard work and dedication paid off when he was named the NFL MVP in 1977. His talent and leadership made him a hero to many fans.

Walter's influence on football goes beyond his records and awards. He inspired many young players to chase their dreams. Walter was also known for his kindness and generosity. He started the Walter Payton Foundation to help kids in need. Walter's efforts off the field showed that he cared about making the world a better place. He raised awareness for organ donation and helped many people through his work. Walter's legacy lives on through the Walter Payton NFL Man of the Year Award. This award is given to players who show excellence on and off the field.

Walter Payton's story is one of hard work, talent, and kindness. He showed that with determination, you can achieve great things. Walter's journey from a small town in Mississippi to becoming one of the greatest football players of all time is truly inspiring. His legacy continues to inspire new generations of football players and fans.

VINCE LOMBARDI AND HIS LEGENDARY COACHING CAREER

Vince Lombardi's path to becoming a legendary coach began at Fordham University in 1947. He started as an assistant coach, learning the ropes and developing his skills. His passion for football was clear, and he worked hard to make a name for himself. Lombardi's big break came when he joined the New York Giants as the offensive coordinator in 1954. He transformed their offense, making it one of the most effective in the league. His innovative strategies and deep under-standing of the game impressed everyone around him. Lombardi's success with the Giants set the stage for his next big opportunity.

When Lombardi became the head coach of the Green Bay Packers in 1959, he changed the team's fortunes. The Packers were struggling, but Lombardi had a plan. He led the Packers to five NFL Championships and the first two Super Bowls. His famous "Packers Sweep" play became a key part of their success. It involved perfect timing and teamwork, allowing the Packers to dominate their opponents. Lombardi's coaching style was a mix of discipline, hard work, and execu-tion. He believed in pushing his players to be the best they could be. His famous quote, "Winning isn't everything; it's the only thing," showed his dedication to success.

Lombardi's leadership style made him a successful and influential coach. He demanded excellence from his players, but he also inspired them. His emphasis on discipline and hard work created a winning culture. Lombardi's ability to motivate his team was unmatched. He knew how to get the best out of each player, turning them into champions. His influence extended beyond the football field. The Super Bowl trophy is named in his honor, a testament to his impact on the game. Future generations of coaches and players look up to Lombardi as a model of excellence and leadership.

THE INSPIRATIONAL STORY OF JERRY RICE

Growing up in Starkville, Mississippi in the 1960s and 70s, Jerry Rice didn't have much, but he had a love for sports. His dad was a brick mason, and Jerry often helped him. This work made Jerry strong and determined. He went to Mississippi Valley State University, where he played college football. Jerry was not the fastest player, but his hard work and skill made him a standout. He set many records and caught the attention of NFL scouts.

When Jerry joined the NFL in 1985, he played for the San Francisco 49ers. His career was full of amazing achievements. He set records for the most career receptions at 1,549, receiving yards at 22,895, and touchdown receptions at 197. Jerry's talent helped the 49ers win three Super Bowl titles. His ability to catch difficult passes and run precise routes made him one of the best wide receivers ever. Fans and players admired his dedication and skill.

Jerry faced many challenges. Some people doubted his

speed and ability to succeed in the NFL. He proved them wrong with his rigorous training. One of his famous workouts was running up a steep hill, known as "The Hill." This training made him faster and stronger. Jerry's hard work and determination helped him overcome any doubts about his capabilities.

Jerry's legacy in football is unmatched. He was inducted into the Pro Football Hall of Fame in 2010, recognizing his incredible career. Even after retiring, Jerry stayed involved in football. He became a mentor and analyst, sharing his knowledge with young players. Jerry Rice's story shows that hard work, determination, and perseverance can lead to greatness. His influence on football continues to inspire players and fans.

LAWRENCE TAYLOR AND THE EVOLUTION OF DEFENSE

Lawrence Taylor, often called "L.T.," is considered by many to be the greatest defensive player in NFL history. His speed, power, and ability to disrupt offenses changed how the outside linebacker position was played. Before Taylor, linebackers mainly focused on tackling and covering receivers. But Taylor brought something new. He was fast and strong enough to rush the quarterback, making it hard for offenses to plan against him. His unique style forced teams to change their strategies. Coaches had to find new ways to protect their quarterbacks from Taylor's relentless attacks.

Taylor's impact on the game is evident in his record-breaking achievements. In 1986, he won the NFL MVP award, a rare honor for a defensive player. This award usually goes to quarterbacks or running backs, but Taylor's performance that season was too incredible to ignore. He helped lead the New York Giants to two Super Bowl victories, showing his ability to perform in the biggest games. Over his career, Taylor recorded 142 sacks and 1,089 tackles. These numbers are amazing and show how dominant he was on the field. His presence alone could change the outcome of a game.

Taylor's influence went beyond his stats. He inspired a new generation of defensive players to be more aggressive and versatile. Coaches began to use linebackers in more creative ways, thanks to Taylor's example. He showed that a linebacker could be the most important player on the field. Taylor's legacy lives on in the way the position is played today. His ability to disrupt offenses and make game-changing plays set a new standard for defensive excellence.

REGGIE WHITE'S UNSTOPPABLE LEGACY

Reggie White, known as the "Minister of Defense," was a force on the football field. He combined size, speed, and technique to dominate his opponents. Standing at 6 feet 5 inches and weighing 291 pounds, Reggie could outmuscle and outrun almost anyone. His ability to get to the quarterback was unmatched. He played with such intensity that offensive lines struggled to contain him. Reggie's presence on the defensive line made life difficult for every quarterback he faced. His skills and determination set him apart as one of the best defensive linemen in football history.

Throughout his career, Reggie achieved many remarkable milestones. He was named the NFL Defensive Player of the Year twice, showcasing his dominance on the field. Reggie played a crucial role in helping the Green Bay Packers win Super Bowl XXXI. His leadership and performance were key to their success. By the time he retired in 2000, Reggie had recorded 198 sacks, making him the NFL's all-time sack leader at that point. He also made 1,111 tackles, further proving his impact on the game. His stats alone tell the story of a player who was relentless and unstoppable.

Reggie's influence extended beyond his on-field achievements. He was a leader and a role model for many young players. His work ethic and dedication inspired others to strive for greatness. Off the field, Reggie was known for his strong character and generosity. He used his platform to make a positive impact in his community. Reggie's legacy lives on through the many players he inspired and the fans who admired his greatness. His combination of talent, determination, and kindness made him a true legend in the world of football.

PRIME TIME: DEION SANDERS AND THE ART OF SHOW-STOPPING DEFENSE

Deion "Prime Time" Sanders is often called the greatest cover cornerback in NFL history. Imagine a player so fast and skillful that he could shut down the best receivers in the league. That's Deion. He had incredible speed and amazing playmaking ability. When he was on the field, quarterbacks avoided throwing in his direction. If they did, they often regretted it. Deion could intercept passes and return them for touchdowns. But that wasn't all. He was also a dynamic return specialist. He could take a punt or kickoff and turn it into a spectacular touchdown.

Deion's career is filled with record-breaking achievements. He won two Super Bowl titles and was selected to the Pro Bowl eight times. He intercepted 53 passes and scored 10 defensive touchdowns by the time he retired from the NFL in 2005. But his skills weren't limited to just defense. Deion also returned nine punts and kickoffs for touchdowns. His ability to change the game in an instant made him a fan favorite. When he stepped onto the field, everyone knew something exciting could happen. His flashy style and confidence earned him the nickname "Prime Time." He loved to entertain the fans and did it with flair.

Deion's impact on the game goes beyond his stats. He redefined what it meant to be a cornerback. His speed and agility forced teams to rethink their strategies. Coaches had to find new ways to deal with his presence on the field. Deion's influence is still seen in today's game. Young players look up to him and try to emulate his style. His legacy as one of the greatest defensive players continues to inspire and excite football fans everywhere.

PEYTON MANNING: THE CEREBRAL QUARTERBACK

Peyton Manning grew up in a football family. His father, Archie Manning, was a famous NFL quarterback. Peyton's younger brother, Eli Manning, also became a star quarterback. Football was a big part of their lives. They would practice together in their backyard. Peyton played high school football at Isidore Newman School in New Orleans. He was a standout player. He threw many touchdowns and led his team to victories. Colleges noticed his talent. He chose to play for the University of Tennessee. At Tennessee, Peyton broke many records and became one of the best college quarterbacks.

Peyton's NFL career was amazing. He was drafted first

overall by the Indianapolis Colts in 1998. Peyton quickly became a star. He led the Colts to many wins and broke several records. He won his first Super Bowl with the Colts in 2007. Later, he joined the Denver Broncos. With the Broncos, he won another Super Bowl in 2016. Peyton set records for career touchdown passes and single-season passing yards. He was named NFL MVP five times. His achievements made him one of the greatest quarterbacks ever.

What set Peyton apart was his intelligence and preparation. He studied game film for hours. He knew every detail about his opponents. On the field, he was famous for his audibles. He would shout "Omaha" to change plays at the line of scrimmage. This confused defenses and gave his team an advantage. Peyton's ability to read defenses and make quick decisions was unmatched.

After retiring, Peyton continued to impact football. He became a popular broadcaster and analyst. He shared his knowledge of the game with fans. Peyton also gave back to the community. He started youth football programs and supported many charities. His work off the field showed his commitment to helping others. Peyton Manning's legacy goes beyond his records and awards. His dedication, intelligence, and generosity make him a true legend.

BO JACKSON: REDEFINING WHAT'S POSSIBLE

Bo Jackson's story is one of overcoming challenges, embracing versatility, and redefining what's possible. Growing up in Alabama in the 1960s and 1970s, Bo faced numerous obstacles, including a tough upbringing and a speech impediment—he had a stutter that made communication difficult. Despite this, Bo found a way to channel his energy and focus through sports. Instead of letting his stutter hold him back, Bo turned to physical activity, where he felt more comfortable expressing himself. His dedication and hard work in both football and baseball allowed him to succeed, showing that overcoming personal challenges can lead to greatness in unexpected ways.

Bo became a star not just in one, but two major professional sports. In the NFL, his speed and power made him one of the most feared running backs in the league. In MLB, his ability to hit home runs and make amazing defensive plays in the outfield earned him a spot in the All-Star Game. Though some believed he should only focus on one sport, Bo proved that dedication and belief in yourself can open up multiple paths to success, even if people around you think it's impossible. He is the only athlete to be named an All-Star in both Major Leaguee Baseball and the National Football League.

Even after suffering a serious hip injury, Bo didn't let adversity stop him. His football career came to an end, but his resilience allowed him to continue playing baseball, even after undergoing hip replacement surgery. Bo's comeback highlights his inner strength and determination. He showed that setbacks, whether physical or personal, do not have to define you.

Bo Jackson's journey, including his battle with stuttering, is a powerful example to young readers that greatness comes from not only what you achieve but how you overcome the challenges along the way. He teaches us that obstacles can be turned into strengths, and with hard work, perseverance, and the courage to follow your passions, you can achieve extraordinary things, no matter what difficulties you face.

TOM BRADY'S RECORD-BREAKING CAREER

Tom Brady grew up in San Mateo, California. In high school, he loved playing football but wasn't noticed by many college scouts. Despite being overlooked, Tom kept working hard. He joined the University of Michigan football team. At Michigan, he faced many challenges but never gave up. He worked his way up from being a backup to the starting quarterback. He led his team to a big win in the Orange Bowl. His college career showed everyone his determination and skill.

In 2000, Tom entered the NFL Draft. He was picked 199th overall by the New England Patriots. Being drafted so low was tough, but Tom used it as motivation. He started as a backup but got his chance when the starting quarterback, Drew Bledsoe, got hurt in 2001. Tom stepped in and led the Patriots to victory. He proved he was ready for the big stage. His early challenges made him stronger and more determined to succeed.

Tom's NFL career is full of amazing records and achievements, which is why he had been referred to as the GOAT, or Greatest of All Time, in recent history. He won seven Super Bowls, more than any other player. He set records for the most career touchdown passes at 649 and the most passing yards at 89,214. He earned multiple NFL MVP awards (9), showing his dominance on the field. Fans and players admired his skills and leadership. Each season, he continued to break records and set new standards.

One reason for Tom's success is his incredible work ethic and leadership. He always prepared for games by studying and practicing. Tom inspired his teammates to do their best. He led by example, showing that hard work pays off. His dedication to fitness and training kept him at the top of his game. Tom's ability to stay calm under pressure and make smart decisions made him a great leader.

MODERN LEGENDS: PATRICK MAHOMES

Patrick Mahomes grew up in a family that loved sports. His dad, Pat Mahomes, was a professional baseball player. This meant Patrick spent a lot of time around athletes. He learned about hard work and dedication early on. In high school, Patrick played both football and baseball. He was good at both but decided to focus on football. He became the quarterback for his high school team and showed everyone his amazing talent. Colleges noticed him quickly. Patrick chose to play football at Texas Tech University.

At Texas Tech, Patrick became known for his strong arm and quick thinking. He threw for many yards and scored lots of touchdowns. His exciting play style made him a fan favorite. Patrick set records and earned awards, proving he was ready for the next level. The NFL took notice, and in 2017, the Kansas City Chiefs drafted him 10th overall. This was a big moment for Patrick. He knew it was time to show the world what he could do.

Patrick's impact on the NFL was immediate. In his first season as a starter, he won the NFL MVP award. He threw for over 5,000 yards and 50 touchdowns. His performance was incredible. Fans and players were amazed by his skills. Patrick didn't stop there. He has led the Chiefs to victory in two Super Bowls as of the writing of this book. He was named the Super Bowl MVP in 2020 and in 2023, showing he could perform on the biggest stage. Patrick also set the record for passing yards in one season in 2022 at 1,057. And his achievements keep growing.

What sets Patrick apart is his unique playing style. He can throw the ball from different angles and make plays on the run. His ability to read defenses and make quick decisions makes him a special player. Patrick's influence on the game is huge. Young players look up to him and try to play like him. His exciting style has made football even more fun to watch.

HARD-HITTING EXCELLENCE: RONNIE LOTT AND THE HEART OF DEFENSIVE GREATNESS

When you think of a football player who could change the game with one hit, you think of Ronnie Lott. Regarded as one of the hardest-hitting safeties in NFL history, Lott made a name for himself with his fierce playing style. He played a key role in the San Francisco 49ers' dynasty during the 1980s. His ability to make game-changing plays helped the 49ers win four Super Bowls. Lott's versatility was impressive. He played both cornerback and safety, showing his adaptability and skill. Whether intercepting a pass or forcing a fumble, Lott was always in the thick of the action.

Lott's accomplishments on the field are remarkable. He recorded 63 interceptions and forced 16 fumbles throughout his career. These stats highlight his knack for making big plays when his team needed them most. Lott's hard-hitting style and football intelligence made him a nightmare for opposing offenses. Quarterbacks had to think twice before throwing in his direction. His ability to read plays and react quickly set him apart from other players. Lott's presence on the field was a game-changer, and his stats reflect his impact.

Beyond his stats, Lott's leadership and determination were unmatched. He played through injuries, showing incredible toughness. In one famous instance, he had the tip of his finger amputated so he could keep playing. His dedication to the game inspired his teammates and fans alike. Lott's influence extended off the field as well. He was known for his leadership and commitment to his community. His work ethic and passion for football left a lasting legacy, making him one of the greatest defensive players in NFL history.

Ronnie Lott's story is a testament to hard work, toughness, and leadership. His impact on the game and his incredible stats make him a true football legend. As we explore more about football, remember the greats like Lott who set the standards for excellence.

Next, we will dive into the rules and strategies that shape the game.

––––––––

CHAPTER 3
UNDERSTANDING THE GAME: RULES AND STRATEGIES

Imagine you are standing on a football field, the sun shining bright, and the crowd cheering. The excitement in the air is electric. This is where the magic happens. Football is more than just a game; it's a thrilling adventure where every play counts. Let's dive into the basic rules and strategies that make this game so special.

BASIC RULES OF FOOTBALL

The main goal in football is to score more points than the other team. So the objective is simple, but it is anything but simple to pull off! Each team tries to move the ball down the field and get it into the end zone. When a player carries or catches the ball in the opponent's end zone, it's called a touchdown, which is worth six points. After a touchdown, the team can kick the ball through the goalposts for an extra point or try to run or pass the ball into the end zone again for two points. Another way to score is by kicking a field goal, which is worth three points. If the defense tackles the offensive player with the ball in their own end zone, it's called a safety, and it's worth two points.

A football game consists of four quarters, each lasting 15 minutes. At the end of the second quarter, there is a halftime break, giving players a chance to rest and strategize. If the game is tied at the end of the fourth quarter, it goes into over-time. In overtime, the first team to score wins, but if no one scores, the game can end in a tie during regular season games.

The football field is 120 yards long and 53.3 yards wide. The field is divided into two main areas, the playing field and the end zones. Each end zone is 10 yards deep and located at the ends of the field. The goalposts are located at the back of each end zone. The field has many markings, including yard lines that run the width of the field every five yards, helping players and referees see how far the ball has moved. The line of scrimmage is an important line where each play starts. The ball is placed on this line, and the teams line up on either side.

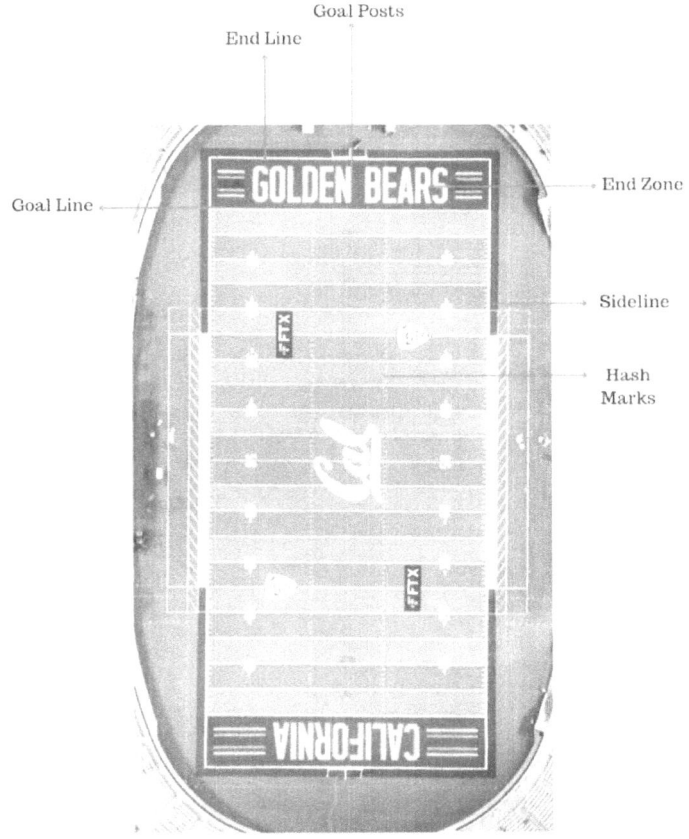

To play the game, each team has an offense and a defense. The offense tries to move the ball down the field by running with it or passing it. The defense tries to stop the offense from moving the ball. The game starts with a snap, where the center gives the ball to the quarterback. The quarterback then decides whether to throw the ball, hand it off to a running back, or run with it himself. Players on the offense work together to block defenders and create paths for the ball carrier.

The offense has four chances, called downs, to move the ball at least ten yards. If they succeed, they get a new set of four downs. If they don't, the other team gets the ball. This makes every down important. Teams often use different strategies on each down to keep the defense guessing. Running the ball is a safer play, while passing can gain more yards but is riskier because the other team had a chance to snatch the ball out of the air.

Some key terms you will hear in football include "snap," "tackle," "fumble," and "interception." A snap is when the center hands or throws the ball to the quarterback to start a play. A tackle is when a defensive player stops the ball carrier by knocking them to the ground. A fumble happens when a player drops the ball, and either team can pick it up, also known as recovering the ball. An interception is when a defensive player catches a pass meant for an offensive player, gaining possession of the ball for their team.

The play clock and game clock are also important. The play clock counts down the time the offense has to start the next play, usually 40 seconds. The game clock keeps track of the overall time left in each quarter. Managing these clocks is a crucial part of the game, as teams need to use their time wisely to score points.

OFFENSIVE AND DEFENSIVE FORMATIONS

Offensive formations are like the starting positions of a chess game. They set the stage for the action to come. One common formation is the I-formation. In this setup, the quarterback stands behind the center, with a fullback and a running back lined up directly behind him, forming a straight line or an "I" shape. This formation is great for running plays because the fullback can block for the running back. It's often used in short-yardage situations where the team needs just a few yards to get a first down.

Another popular formation is the shotgun formation. Here, the quarterback stands several yards behind the center. This gives him more time to see the field and make decisions. The shotgun formation is useful for passing plays because it allows the quarterback to quickly read the defense and throw the ball. It's often used in situations where the team needs to gain a lot of yards, like third and long. Third and long refers to a situation where the offensive team is on third down and needs to gain a significant number of yards, usually 7 or more, to acheive a first down. The single-back formation, on the other hand, involves only one running back lined up behind the quarterback. This formation spreads out the defense and is good for both running and passing plays. It's versatile and can keep the defense guessing.

On the defensive side, formations are just as important. The 4-3 defense is one of the most common setups. It features four defensive linemen, who line up on the line of scrimmage, and three linebackers. The linemen try to break through the offensive line to tackle the ball carrier or sack the quarterback. The linebackers support the linemen and cover the middle of the field. This formation is balanced and can defend against both running and passing plays. The 3-4 defense, with three linemen and four linebackers, is another strategy. The extra linebacker can be used to blitz, or rush the quarterback, adding more pressure. This formation is flexible and can confuse the offense with different blitzing schemes.

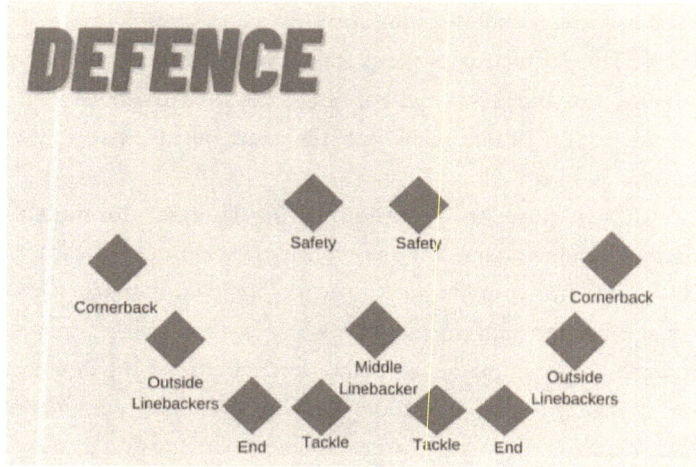

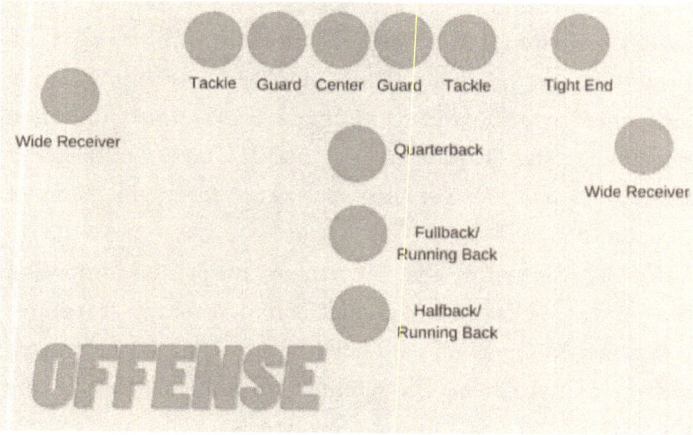

The nickel defense is a special formation used mainly to defend against passing plays. It includes five defensive backs instead of the usual four. The extra defensive back, called the nickelback, helps cover additional receivers. This formation is effective against teams that like to throw the ball a lot. It's often used in obvious passing situations, like third and long.

Each defensive formation is designed to counter specific offensive strategies, making the game a constant battle of wits.

In these formations, every player has a specific role. On offense, the quarterback is the leader. He decides whether to pass, hand off for a run play, or run with the ball himself. The running back's job is to carry the ball after the quarterback hands it off to him and try to gain yards. Wide receivers run routes to catch passes and help block defenders for running plays. The linemen, including the center, guards, and tackles, protect the quarterback and open paths for the running back. The tight end is a mix of a lineman and receiver. He blocks and catches passes, making him a versatile player. Today, famous tight ends include Rob Gronkowski, Travis Kelce, Georg Kittle, and Mark Andrews.

On defense, linemen rush the quarterback and stop running plays. Linebackers cover a lot of ground. They tackle ball carriers, defend against passes, and sometimes blitz. Defensive backs, including cornerbacks and safeties, cover receivers and try to intercept passes. Each player must work together to stop the offense and get the ball back for their team.

Formations play a huge role in the strategy of football. Offensive formations can exploit defensive weaknesses. For example, spreading out the defense with multiple wide receivers can create running lanes where there is more room for players to catch a pass. Pre-snap movements, like shifting players or sending a receiver in motion, can reveal the defense's plans. Audibles, or last-second changes by the quarterback to the planned play, can adjust the play to counter the defense. Defensive formations, on the other hand, aim to confuse and disrupt the offense. Blitzes from unexpected players can force the quarterback into making mistakes. Coverage schemes can take away the offense's favorite passing options.

POSITIONAL UNIFORM NUMBERS

A player's number is more than a number—it is tied to their position. In the NFL, certain numbers indicate certain positions, as this helps the referee determine who is and who isn't allowed to catch the ball. The following numbers are worn by specific positions:

- 0 to 19 are worn by quarterbacks
- 0 to 49 and 90 to 99 are worn by punters and kickers
- 0 to 49 are reserved for defensive backs
- 0 to 49 and 80 to 89 are reserved for running backs
- 0 to 49 and 80 to 89 are worn by tight ends
- 0 to 49 and 80 to 89 are reserved for offensive lineman
- 0 to 59 and 90 to 99 are worn by linebackers
- 50 to 79 are reserved for offensive lineman
- 50 to 79 and 90 to 99 are worn by defensive linemen

These jersey numbers are the official position numbers as of the 2024 season.

THE ROLE OF THE QUARTERBACK

The quarterback is often seen as the most crucial player on the field. This is because they have many important duties. The quarterback leads the team on and off the field. They need to inspire their teammates and keep them focused. During the game, the quarterback makes quick decisions. Their choices can change the outcome of the game. Leadership and decision-making are key to a quarterback's role. They need to stay calm under pressure and guide their team through tough situations.

Successful quarterbacks have certain skills and attributes. They need strong arms to throw the ball far and accurately. Arm strength helps them make long passes, while accuracy ensures the ball reaches the receiver. Mobility is also important. Some plays require the quarterback to move around to avoid defenders. Being able to read defenses is another crucial skill. Quarterbacks must quickly see how the defense is set up and adjust their plans. This helps them make smart decisions and find open teammates. These skills come from lots of practice and studying the game.

The quarterback has many responsibilities during a game. They start by calling the snap count, which signals the center to snap the ball. Handling the snap is important, as a bad snap can ruin a play. Before the snap, the quarterback makes pre-snap reads. They look at the defense and may call an audible to change the play. This helps the offense adapt to what the defense is doing. Once the play starts, the quarterback executes it by passing, running, or handing off the ball. Each play requires focus and quick thinking.

Different quarterbacks have unique playing styles. Peyton Manning is known for his precision and football IQ. He spent hours studying game film and knew every detail about his opponents. On the field, he made quick decisions and accurate throws. His ability to read defenses and adjust plays made him a top quarterback. In contrast, Michael Vick was famous for his athleticism and dual-threat capability. He could throw long passes and run fast, making him hard to stop. Vick's style brought excitement to the game and changed how people viewed quarterbacks.

The history of the dual-threat quarterback goes back to players like Fran Tarkenton. In the 1960s and 1970s, Tarkenton was known for his ability to run and pass. He often scrambled out of the pocket to avoid sacks and make plays. This was not a common attribute for quarterbacks at this time in history. His style laid the foundation for future dual-threat quarterbacks. Players like Vick built on this legacy, showing that quarterbacks could be dangerous runners and passers. Today, many quarterbacks combine these skills to keep defenses guessing.

Being a quarterback is not easy. It requires leadership, quick thinking, and a mix of skills. The quarterback's role is crucial to a team's success. They must inspire their teammates, make smart decisions, and execute plays effectively. Whether it's through precision passing or athletic runs, quarterbacks have different styles that make them unique. Their impact on the game is huge, and they play a key role in every team's strategy.

UNDERSTANDING SPECIAL TEAMS

Special teams play a crucial role in football. They handle kick-offs, punts, and field goals. These plays can change the game by affecting field position and scoring opportunities. Think of special teams as the unit that sets the stage for the offense and defense. When a game starts or a team scores, the special teams take the field. They kick the ball to the opposing team, hoping to pin them deep in their own territory. A great kickoff can make it harder for the other team to score. Special teams also come into play when a team decides to punt the ball on fourth down. The goal is to kick the ball far downfield, forcing the other team to start their drive from a tough spot. Field goals and extra points are other key duties of special teams. These kicks can add valuable points to the score.

Within special teams, each player has a specific job. The kicker is responsible for kicking field goals, extra points, and kickoffs. The punter, on the other hand, kicks the ball during punts. The long snapper is crucial for getting the ball to the punter or holder quickly and accurately. Return specialists are the players who catch the ball during kickoffs and punts and try to run it back for as many yards as possible. Coverage teams have the job of tackling the return specialist and stopping their progress. Blocking assignments are also vital. Players must protect the kicker or punter from defenders trying to block the kick.

Special teams execute several key plays in a game. One of the most exciting plays is the kickoff. The kicker boots the ball downfield, and the opposing team's return specialist catches it. They then try to run as far as they can before being tackled. Kickoff returns can lead to big plays and sometimes even touchdowns. Another common play is the field goal attempt. When a team is close to the end zone but can't score a touchdown, they may try to kick a field goal for three points. Extra points happen after a touchdown, where the kicker tries to add one more point by kicking the ball through the goalposts. Punts are another important special teams play. When a team can't get a first down, they punt the ball to push the opposing team back. Punt returns can also lead to exciting moments, as the return specialist tries to gain yards or even score.

Strategies for special teams vary depending on the game situation. One interesting strategy is the onside kick. This is a short kickoff designed to give the kicking team a chance to recover the ball. It's often used late in the game when a team is behind and needs to get the ball back quickly. Another tactic is the fake punt or field goal. In these plays, the team pretends to kick but instead tries to run or pass the ball for a first down. These surprise plays can catch the opponent off guard and keep the drive alive.

Special teams can make or break a game. Their role in kickoffs, punts, and field goals is vital. Each position, from the kicker to the long snapper, has specific duties that contribute to the team's success. Common plays like kickoffs, field goals, and punts are exciting and can change the game's momentum. Special teams strategies, like onside kicks and fake punts, add an element of surprise. Understanding special teams helps you see how every part of the game works together.

COMMON FOOTBALL PENALTIES

Penalties play a vital role in football. They ensure that the game is fair and safe for everyone. Referees are in charge of spotting and calling these penalties. You can recognize them on the field by their striped shirts and whistles. When a player breaks a rule, the referee throws a yellow flag onto the field. This signals that a penalty has occurred. Penalties can change the flow of the game. They can push a team backward or give the other team an advantage. Understanding these penalties helps players and fans appreciate the game's strategy and fairness.

Some penalties mainly affect the offensive team. One common penalty is holding. This happens when an offensive player grabs and holds a defender to prevent them from reaching the ball carrier. Holding usually results in a ten-yard penalty against the offense. Another penalty is a false start. This occurs when an offensive player moves before the ball is snapped. It results in a five-yard penalty. An illegal formation is another offense. This happens when the offensive team does not have the required number of players on the line of scrimmage. This penalty also results in a five-yard loss. These penalties can make it harder for the offense to move the ball and score points.

Defensive penalties can also have a big impact on the game. Pass interference is one of these. It happens when a defensive player makes illegal contact with a receiver before the ball arrives. This penalty results in the offense gaining the spot of the foul or an automatic first down. Another common penalty is offsides. This occurs when a defensive player crosses the line of scrimmage before the ball is snapped. It results in a five-yard penalty against the defense. Roughing the passer is a serious penalty. It happens when a defensive player makes illegal contact with the quarterback after they have thrown the ball, such as a late hit, a high hit, or driving the quarterback into the ground. This penalty results in a fifteen-yard penalty and an automatic first down. Defensive penalties can extend the offense's drive and make it easier for them to score.

Personal fouls and unsportsmanlike conduct are penalties related to player behavior and safety. Personal fouls include actions like face masks, where a player grabs an opponent's face mask, and unnecessary roughness, where a player makes a tackle or hit that is too aggressive. These penalties usually result in a fifteen-yard penalty. Unsportsmanlike conduct involves actions that show poor sportsmanship, such as taunting or celebrating excessively. This penalty also results in a fifteen-yard loss. These penalties are meant to keep the game safe and respectful.

Understanding football penalties is important for players and fans. Penalties ensure that everyone follows the rules and plays fairly. They can change the outcome of a game by giving one team an advantage or pushing the other team back. Knowing these penalties helps you appreciate the strategy behind every play and the importance of playing by the rules.

THE IMPORTANCE OF GAME FILM AND ANALYSIS

Imagine you are on a football team getting ready for a big game. One of the most important tools your team will use is game film. Coaches and players watch videos of past games to see how the other team plays. They study the opponents tendencies and formations. This means they look for patterns in how the other team lines up and what plays they run. By doing this, they can find weaknesses to exploit. Maybe the other team has trouble stopping long passes, or perhaps they always run to the right on third down. Knowing these tendencies helps your team make a game plan.

Video analysts play a key role in this process. Their job is to watch hours of game film and break it down into manageable parts. They create clips of different plays and formations. This makes it easier for coaches and players to study the film without watching entire games. Analysts also create scouting reports. These reports highlight the strengths and weaknesses of the opponents. They provide detailed information that coaches use to develop strategies. For example, a scouting report might note that the opposing quarterback struggles when pressured. The coach can then plan more blitzes to take advantage of this.

Watching film is not just about studying the opponent. It also helps players improve their own performance. Players can see what they did well and what they need to work on. Maybe a player notices that they missed a block or took a bad angle on a tackle. By seeing these mistakes, they can make adjustments and improve. Film study also helps players learn from their successes. They can see what techniques worked and try to repeat them. This continuous learning helps players get better each week.

Some players are famous for their dedication to film study. Peyton Manning, for example, was known for his meticulous preparation. He spent hours watching film, learning every detail about the defenses he would face. This preparation helped him make quick decisions on the field. Ray Lewis, a legendary linebacker, also used film study to his advantage. He watched film to anticipate the offense's plays. This allowed him to be in the right place at the right time. His ability to read the offense and make plays was a big reason for his success.

Game film and analysis are crucial for football teams. They help coaches and players prepare for upcoming games by studying the opponents' tendencies and formations. Video analysts break down the film into clips and create scouting reports. This information helps teams develop game plans. Watching film also helps players improve their own performance by learning from their mistakes and successes. Players like Peyton Manning and Ray Lewis showed how important film study can be. Their dedication to preparation made them some of the best players in football history.

Game film and analysis are vital tools that help teams win. They provide the information needed to develop strategies and improve performance. As you learn more about football, remember the importance of preparation and study. These tools can make a big difference on the field.

———

CHAPTER 4
FOOTBALL SKILLS AND DRILLS

I magine you're on the field, the sun shining down, and you have the football in your hands. You hear the crowd cheering and your teammates shouting encouragement. This is where you get to show your skills. But before you can throw that perfect pass or make that amazing play, you need to practice. And practice starts with drills. Drills help you improve your skills and become a better player. Let's dive into some drills that will help you become a better quarterback.

DRILLS TO IMPROVE PASSING ACCURACY

Warming up is very important before you start any drills. It helps prevent injuries and gets your body ready for action. Start with some arm circles. Hold your arms out to the sides and make small circles. This helps loosen up your shoulder muscles. Next, try some shoulder stretches. Reach one arm across your chest and use your other arm to gently pull it closer. Switch arms and repeat. These stretches will help you avoid muscle strains. After stretching, do some light tossing. Stand a few yards away from a partner and gently toss the football back and forth. This helps build up your arm strength gradually.

Now that you're warmed up, it's time to work on your passing accuracy. One great way to do this is by using target passing drills. Set up some cones or buckets at different distances and angles. Aim for these targets as you throw the football. Start with the closest target and work your way to the farthest one. This will help you improve your aim and control. For an added challenge, have a partner move the targets around. Try to hit the moving targets. This simulates real-game situations where your receiver is always on the move.

Footwork is crucial for accurate passing. Without good footwork, even the strongest arm won't help. Practice three-step and five-step drop-backs. Start by standing behind the line of scrimmage. Take three quick steps back, plant your back foot, and then throw the ball. For the five-step drop-back, take five steps instead. This drill helps you get into the right position to throw. Focus on planting your foot firmly before you release the ball. Another useful drill is the plant and throw. Stand still, then quickly plant your foot and throw. This helps you practice setting your feet quickly and throwing accurately.

Situational passing drills are also very helpful. They mimic real-game scenarios and improve your decision-making. Try rolling out to the left and right. Start by standing behind the line of scrimmage. Take a few steps to your left, then throw the ball. Repeat the drill, but this time roll out to your right. This helps you practice throwing on the move. It's important to keep your eyes on your target and throw accurately even when you're not standing still. Another good drill is the quick release under pressure. Have a partner act as a defender and rush towards you. Try to release the ball quickly before they reach you. This drill helps you stay calm and make quick decisions under pressure.

Improving your passing accuracy takes practice and dedication. Warm-up exercises help prevent injuries and get your body ready. Target passing drills improve your aim and control. Footwork drills help you get into the right position to throw accurately. Situational passing drills mimic real-game scenarios and improve your decision-making. By practicing these drills regularly, you will become a better quarterback. You will be able to throw accurate passes and make smart decisions on the field. Remember, practice makes perfect!

MASTERING THE ART OF TACKLING

Tackling is one of the most important skills in football. It can stop a player in their tracks and change the momentum of the game. But it's also important to tackle safely. Keeping your head up is crucial. When you keep your head up, you can see where you are going and avoid injuries. Instead of using your head, you should use your shoulder to make contact. This method is safer and just as effective. Once you make contact, wrap your arms around the ball carrier. Drive through the tackle by pushing with your legs. This helps bring the player down and stops their forward progress. Practicing these fundamentals ensures you tackle safely and effectively.

To practice form tackling, you can use tackling dummies and sleds. Tackling dummies are padded and can stand upright. They are perfect for practicing your form. Run towards the dummy, keep your head up, and use your shoulder to make contact. Wrap your arms around the dummy and drive through it. Sleds are another great tool. They are heavier and can slide along the ground. Tackling a sled helps you practice driving through the tackle. Partner drills with controlled contact are also helpful. Pair up with a teammate and practice tackling each other. Take turns being the tackler and the ball carrier. Make sure to keep the contact light and focus on good form.

Open-field tackling is a bit different. It happens when you need to tackle a player who has a lot of space to move. Angle tackling drills are perfect for this. Set up cones to create a path. Have a teammate run along this path while you try to tackle them. Approach from an angle, keeping your head up and using your shoulder. This helps you practice closing the distance and making the tackle. Sideline containment exercises are also useful. In these drills, you try to tackle a player running along the sideline. Your goal is to keep them from turning upfield. Use the sideline as a boundary to help you contain the player.

Improving your tackling strength and technique is important too. Squats and lunges are great exercises for building lower body strength. They work your legs and help you drive through tackles. Stand with your feet shoulder-width apart and lower your body into a squat. Keep your back straight and push through your heels to stand back up. Lunges are similar. Step forward with one leg and lower your body until your back knee nearly touches the ground. Push back up to the starting position and switch legs. Core exercises help with stability and balance. Planks are a great core exercise. Hold your body in a straight line, supported by your forearms and toes. Hold this position for as long as you can. Another good exercise is the Russian twist. Sit on the ground, lean back slightly, and lift your feet off the ground. Twist your torso from side to side, touching the ground next to you with your hands. These exercises help you stay balanced and stable during tackles.

Tackling is a skill that requires practice and dedication. By focusing on the fundamentals, you can tackle safely and effectively. Practice form tackling with dummies and sleds to get the basics down. Use open-field tackling drills to improve your ability to tackle in space. Build your strength and technique with lower body and core exercises. With practice, you will become a better tackler and a valuable player on your team.

SPEED AND AGILITY DRILLS

Improving your speed and agility can make a big difference in your football performance. One great tool to use is the agility ladder. This simple piece of equipment can help you improve your footwork and quickness. Start with one-foot hops. Place the ladder on the ground and hop forward, landing in each square with one foot. This drill helps you develop balance and control. Next, try two-foot hops. Hop forward with both feet landing together in each square. This drill builds strength and coordination. Another useful drill is the in-and-out ladder drill. Step into a square with both feet, then step out to the sides. Continue this pattern down the ladder. This drill improves your foot speed and agility.

Cone drills are another effective way to enhance your ability to change direction quickly. The "L" drill is a popular choice. Set up three cones in the shape of an "L." Start at the first cone, sprint to the second, then shuffle sideways to the third cone. Finally, backpedal to the first cone. This drill helps you practice quick changes in direction and improves your overall agility. The "T" drill is also useful. Set up four cones in the shape of a "T." Start at the base of the "T," sprint to the top, shuffle sideways to each end, then backpedal to the starting point. This drill helps you develop lateral movement and quick direction changes. Zig-zag cone drills are another great option. Set up cones in a zig-zag pattern and sprint through them, changing direction at each cone. This drill helps you practice sharp turns and quick movements.

Sprinting drills are perfect for boosting your overall speed. Start with 10-yard sprints. Mark a starting point and a finish line 10 yards away. Sprint as fast as you can from the start to the finish. This drill helps you develop explosive speed. Next, try 40-yard sprints. Mark a starting point and a finish line 40 yards away. Sprint as fast as you can over the longer distance. This drill helps you build endurance and sustained speed. Interval training is also very effective. Choose varied distances, like 20 yards, 40 yards, and 60 yards. Sprint each distance, then rest for a short time before sprinting again. This helps you improve both your speed and your ability to recover quickly.

Combining speed and agility drills can give you a comprehensive workout. Shuttle runs are a great way to do this. Set up two cones 10 yards apart. Sprint from one cone to the other, touch the ground, then sprint back. Repeat this pattern several times. This drill helps you practice quick direction changes and builds your overall speed. Reaction drills with a partner are also very useful. Have a partner stand a few yards away and hold a ball. When they drop the ball, sprint to catch it before it hits the ground. This drill helps you practice quick starts and improves your reaction time.

Using an agility ladder can help you improve your footwork. Start with one-foot hops, then move on to two-foot hops. Try the in-and-out ladder drill to build speed. Cone drills like the "L" drill and "T" drill help you change direction quickly. Zig-zag cone drills are also great for practicing sharp turns. Sprinting drills like 10-yard and 40-yard sprints boost your speed. Interval training with varied distances helps build endurance. Combining drills, like shuttle runs and reaction drills, gives you a complete workout. By practicing these drills, you will become faster and more agile on the field.

CATCHING TECHNIQUES FOR WIDE RECEIVERS

Catching a football is one of the most exciting parts of the game. To catch a football effectively, you need to know the basics. Start with proper hand positioning and grip. Place your hands out in front of you, with your fingers spread wide. When a pass is coming in high, use the "diamond" technique. Form a diamond shape by touching your thumbs and pointer fingers together. This helps you catch the ball with your hands instead of your body. Using your hands gives you better control and reduces the chance of the ball bouncing off your chest. Keep your eyes on the ball and follow it all the way into your hands. Once you catch it, secure it by tucking it away against your body safely.

Improving your hand-eye coordination is key to becoming a good receiver. One great exercise is the tennis ball toss. Grab a tennis ball and toss it against a wall. Try to catch it with one hand, then switch to the other hand. This helps you improve your reflexes and coordination. Another fun drill is partner passing. Stand a few yards apart from a friend and pass the football back and forth. Vary the speed and height of your passes to make it more challenging. This drill helps you get used to catching different types of throws. You can also try catching smaller objects like a bean bag or a smaller ball to sharpen your focus.

Route running is a big part of being a wide receiver. Combine your route-running drills with catching to simulate game scenarios. Start with running slants. Begin by standing at the line of scrimmage. On the snap, take a few steps forward, then cut sharply at a 45-degree angle. Look for the pass and catch it while on the move. Next, practice running outs. Run straight ahead for a few yards, then make a sharp turn towards the sideline. Focus on catching the ball as you turn. Go routes are another important route to practice. Sprint straight down the field as fast as you can. Keep your eyes on the quarterback and be ready to catch the long pass. These drills help you practice catching passes while running different routes.

Catching under pressure is a skill that every receiver needs. Practice high-pointing the ball against a defender. Have a friend or coach act as the defender. When the ball is thrown, jump up and try to catch it at the highest point. This helps you win battles for the ball in the air. Another useful drill is catching in traffic. Set up a few cones or have multiple defenders around you. Run through the defenders and focus on catching the ball while avoiding them. This simulates game situations where you have to catch the ball with defenders all around you. Keeping your focus and staying calm is key to making these tough catches.

Being a great wide receiver requires practice and dedication. Start with the basics of proper hand positioning and grip. Use the "diamond" technique for high passes. Improve your hand-eye coordination with tennis ball tosses and partner passing drills. Combine route-running drills with catching to simulate game scenarios. Practice running slants, outs, and go routes. Work on catching under pressure by high-pointing the ball and catching in traffic. Each of these drills helps you become a better receiver. Remember to keep your eyes on the ball, use your hands to catch, and secure the ball once you have it. With practice, you will become a reliable and skilled wide receiver, ready to make big plays on the field.

FOOTWORK DRILLS FOR LINEMEN

Imagine being on the line, ready to block the opponent. Your stance and start are the keys to winning that battle. A proper stance helps you stay balanced and ready to move. There are two main stances: the three-point stance and the four-point stance. In a three-point stance, place one hand on the ground while keeping your other hand free. Bend your knees, and keep your back straight. This stance gives you a good balance and a quick start. In a four-point stance, put both hands on the ground. This stance provides even more stability and is often used by defensive linemen. Once in stance, focus on your first step. A quick first step can give you an edge over your opponent. Practice quick first step drills by pushing off from your stance as fast as you can. This helps build explosive power and speed.

Lateral movement is crucial for linemen. You need to move side to side to block defenders and keep them away from the ball carrier. One effective drill is the slide step. Stand in your stance, then slide your feet to the side without crossing them. Keep your knees bent and stay low. This drill helps you move quickly and stay balanced. Another useful drill is the mirror drill. Pair up with a teammate. One person moves side to side, and the other person mirrors their movements. This drill improves your lateral quickness and reaction time. Blocking sled exercises are also important. Push a blocking sled across the field. This drill helps you practice using your legs and body to move a heavy object, simulating the force needed to block an opponent.

Hand placement and leverage are key to effective blocking. Proper hand placement helps you control the defender. Practice punch and extend drills to improve this skill. Stand in your stance and punch forward with your hands, then extend your arms fully. This helps you create space between you and the defender. Using leverage is also important. Lower your body and use your legs to push the defender up and back. This gives you control and keeps the defender away from the ball carrier. Practice using leverage by pushing against a partner or a blocking dummy. Focus on staying low and using your legs to drive through the block.

Combining footwork with strength training can make you a powerful lineman. Medicine ball throws are a great way to do this. Hold a medicine ball with both hands, then throw it forward as hard as you can. This simulates the force needed for blocking. Another useful exercise is the band-resisted movement drill. Attach a resistance band to a stationary object and loop it around your waist. Practice your blocking movements while the band provides resistance. This helps build strength in your legs and core, making you a more effective blocker.

Improving your footwork and blocking skills takes practice and dedication. Start with the basics of a proper stance and explosive start. Practice quick first step drills to build speed. Use slide steps and mirror drills to improve your lateral movement. Blocking sled exercises help you practice using your body to move a heavy object. Focus on proper hand placement and leverage with punch and extend drills. Use medicine ball throws and band-resisted movement drills to combine footwork with strength training. Each of these drills helps you become a stronger and more effective lineman.

By focusing on these drills, you will improve your footwork and blocking skills. A proper stance and quick start give you an edge over your opponent. Lateral movement helps you stay with the defender and protect the ball carrier. Proper hand placement and leverage give you control. Combining footwork with strength training makes you a powerful blocker. With practice, you will become a valuable asset to your team.

As you work on these drills, remember that practice and dedication are key. Keep pushing yourself to improve, and you will see the results on the field. Every great player was once a beginner - what you do today sets the stage for who you'll become tomorrow. Remember that champions aren't born in stadiums; they're made during the early mornings, the late nights, and every drop of sweat in between. Your effort, not your talent, will determine how far you go. Be the hardest worker in the room.

Next, we will dive into the unforgettable moments in football history, where every skill you've learned comes into play.

———

CHAPTER 5
ICONIC GAMES AND UNFORGETTABLE MOMENTS

P icture this: it's a cold December day in 1972. You're in Pittsburgh, Pennsylvania, and the air is filled with excitement. The Pittsburgh Steelers are facing the Oakland Raiders in a crucial playoff game. The stands are packed with fans bundled up in their winter coats, cheering for their teams. This game is important for both teams. The Steelers are making their second playoff appearance ever, and the Raiders are known for their tough, gritty play. Both teams know that winning this game could lead them closer to the championship.

THE IMMACULATE RECEPTION

The Steelers had a lot on the line. Their coach, Chuck Noll, had worked hard to turn the team into a contender. They had Terry Bradshaw as their quarterback, a young talent known for his strong arm. The Raiders, led by coach John Madden, were equally determined. They had players like Daryle Lamonica, their quarterback, and Jack Tatum, a fierce defender. The game was close from the start, with both teams fighting hard for every yard. As the clock ticked down, the Raiders were leading 7-6. The Steelers had one last chance to win the game. With only 22 seconds left, they faced a fourth-and-10 from their own 40-yard line.

Terry Bradshaw took the snap and dropped back to pass. The Raiders' defenders rushed at him, trying to bring him down. Bradshaw scrambled, looking for an open receiver. He spotted John "Frenchy" Fuqua and threw the ball his way. Just as the ball reached Fuqua, he was hit hard by Raiders' defender Jack Tatum. The impact caused the ball to bounce high into the air. For a split second, it seemed like the game was over. But then, out of nowhere, Franco Harris appeared. He caught the ball just inches above the ground and started running. Harris dodged a few defenders and sprinted into the end zone, scoring a miraculous touchdown. The crowd erupted in cheers, and the Steelers took the lead. They won the game 13-7, thanks to Harris's incredible catch and run.

The Immaculate Reception changed everything for the Steelers. Their victory meant they advanced in the playoffs, giving them a shot at the championship. Players and coaches couldn't believe what had just happened. "It was like a miracle," said Bradshaw. Fans went wild, celebrating what they had just witnessed. The play gave the Steelers a new sense of confidence. It showed them that anything was possible if they never gave up. The excitement from that game carried over into future seasons, helping the Steelers build a winning tradition.

The impact of the Immaculate Reception didn't stop there. It became one of the most talked-about plays in NFL history. People still debate whether the ball touched the ground before Harris caught it. Some say it did, while others believe it didn't. But regardless of the debate, the play is a defining moment in football history. It showed the magic and unpredictability of the game. The Immaculate Reception is celebrated every year, reminding fans of that incredible moment when Franco Harris made an impossible catch. This play helped set the Steelers on a path to future championships and left a lasting legacy in the NFL.

THE MIRACLE AT THE MEADOWLANDS

Imagine you're at Giants Stadium in New Jersey on November 19, 1978. The New York Giants are playing against the Philadelphia Eagles. Both teams are desperate for a win. The Giants haven't made the playoffs in 14 years, and the Eagles are in the middle of a 17-year playoff drought. This game is crucial for both teams' seasons. The crowd is buzzing with excitement and tension. Every play feels like it could change everything.

As the game progresses, the Giants take a small lead. The clock is winding down, and they just need to run out the time to secure their victory. Everyone expects them to play it safe. Usually, teams in this situation take a knee, which means the quarterback simply kneels to the ground to let the clock run out. But for some reason, the Giants decide to run the ball one last time. It's a risky move, but they feel confident.

Joe Pisarcik, the Giants' quarterback, takes the snap and attempts to hand off the ball to running back Larry Csonka. But something goes horribly wrong. The handoff is fumbled, and the ball drops to the ground. The crowd gasps in disbelief. Suddenly, Herman Edwards, a cornerback for the Eagles, scoops up the loose ball. He runs untouched into the end zone for a touchdown. The Eagles take the lead with just seconds left on the clock. The final score is Eagles 19, Giants 17.

The reactions are immediate and intense. On the Giants' sideline, players and coaches are in shock. They can't believe what just happened. Fans in the stands are stunned, some with their hands on their heads in disbelief. On the Eagles' side, it's a different story. Players are jumping up and down, celebrating their unexpected victory. The fans are cheering loudly, realizing they have just witnessed something incredible.

This play, now known as the "Miracle at the Meadowlands," has a lasting impact on football. It changes the way teams handle the final moments of a game. The Giants' mistake shows that even a small risk can lead to a huge loss. To prevent this from happening again, teams start using the "Victory Formation." In this formation, the quarterback takes a knee to safely run out the clock. This simple change becomes a standard practice in football, ensuring that teams can protect their leads without unnecessary risks.

The "Miracle at the Meadowlands" also affects coaching strategies. Coaches become more cautious in the final moments of a game. They focus on securing the win rather than trying to gain a few extra yards. This play serves as a reminder that sometimes, the safest option is the best one. The Giants learn from their mistake and make changes to their coaching staff. They bring in new leaders who help turn the team around in the coming years.

The play also has an emotional impact on fans. For Eagles fans, it becomes a moment of pride and joy. They celebrate the unexpected victory and use it as a rallying point for future success. For Giants fans, it's a painful memory, but one that teaches valuable lessons about the game. The "Miracle at the Meadowlands" becomes a story passed down through generations, a reminder of the unpredictable nature of football.

The "Miracle at the Meadowlands" is more than just a fumble and a recovery. It's a moment that changes the course of football history. It shows the importance of strategy and caution, especially in the final moments of a game. It leaves a lasting legacy that affects how teams play and how coaches make decisions. This unforgettable moment becomes a part of football lore, reminding everyone that in football, anything can happen.

THE MUSIC CITY MIRACLE

Imagine the excitement on January 8, 2000. The Tennessee Titans and the Buffalo Bills were playing in an AFC Wild Card playoff game. Both teams had worked hard all season to get here. The Titans, with a 13-3 record, were looking to continue their strong season. The Bills, with an 11-5 record, were hoping to make a deep playoff run. The game was tight, and every play mattered. As the game neared its end, the Bills led 16-15. The Titans needed a miracle to keep their playoff hopes alive. The crowd was on the edge of their seats, knowing this could be the last play of the game.

The final moments of the game were intense. The Titans lined up for a kickoff return with only 16 seconds left. Special teams coach Alan Lowry called for a play known as "Home Run Throwback." Lorenzo Neal, a strong and reliable player, fielded the short kickoff. He quickly handed the ball to Frank Wycheck, who was positioned to the right. Wycheck then made a bold move. He threw a lateral pass across the field to Kevin Dyson, who caught the ball and started running. The Bills' defenders were caught off guard. Dyson sprinted down the sideline, avoiding tackles and speeding past everyone. He ran 75 yards to the end zone, scoring a touchdown. The crowd went wild as the Titans took the lead, securing a 22-16 victory.

The reactions were immediate and intense. On the Titans' sideline, players and coaches erupted in joy. They hugged, high-fived, and celebrated their miraculous win. Fans in the stands were cheering loudly, some even crying tears of happiness. It was a moment they would never forget. On the Bills' side, there was disbelief and anger. Players and coaches protested, arguing that Wycheck's pass was an illegal forward throw. They believed the play should be reviewed and over-turned. But after reviewing the play, the officials confirmed it was a legal lateral. The touchdown stood, and the game was over.

The Music City Miracle had a huge impact on the Titans' playoff run. The thrilling win boosted their confidence and momentum. They went on to defeat the Indianapolis Colts in the next round. Then, they beat the Jacksonville Jaguars in the AFC Championship game. This incredible playoff run led them to Super Bowl XXXIV. Although they lost to the St. Louis Rams in a close game, the Music City Miracle remained a highlight of their season. It showed the power of teamwork, determination, and never giving up.

The play became an iconic moment in NFL playoff history. Fans and analysts still talk about it today. It is remembered as one of the greatest plays of all time. The Titans' victory inspired other teams to believe in the impossible. The Music City Miracle also highlighted the importance of special teams. It showed how one play could change the outcome of a game. The Titans' legacy was forever changed by that unforgettable moment. The Music

City Miracle is a testament to the excitement and unpredictability of football.

THE GREATEST COMEBACK: BILLS VS. OILERS

The AFC Wild Card game on January 3, 1993, between the
Buffalo Bills and the Houston Oilers, was nothing short of
dramatic. The Oilers came out strong, dominating the first
half. Warren Moon, the Oilers' quarterback, was on fire. He
threw passes with pinpoint accuracy, leading his team to a
commanding lead. The Oilers' defense was just as impressive.
They stopped the Bills at every turn, making it look like an
easy win. By halftime, the Oilers were ahead 28-3. The Bills
were struggling. Their starting quarterback, Jim Kelly, was
injured and couldn't play. Frank Reich, the backup quarterback, had to step in. The Bills' fans were worried. It seemed
like everything was going wrong for their team.

As the second half began, things didn't look any better for
the Bills. The Oilers scored another touchdown, making it 35-
3. But then, something amazing happened. Frank Reich,
known for his calmness under pressure, started to lead a
comeback. He threw a short pass to Kenneth Davis for a
touchdown. The Bills' defense stepped up, forcing the Oilers
to punt. Reich then connected with Don Beebe for another
touchdown. The energy in the stadium changed. Fans started
to believe in their team again.

Andre Reed played a crucial role in the comeback. He
made several key receptions, including three touchdowns.
Each catch brought the Bills closer to the Oilers' lead. The
crowd was going wild. They could feel the momentum shifting. Reich continued to lead with confidence. The Bills scored
again, this time with a one-yard run by Davis. The score was

now 35-31. The Oilers were stunned. They tried to hold on, but the Bills were unstoppable. With just over three minutes left, Reich threw another touchdown pass to Reed. The Bills took the lead for the first time in the game, making it 38-35.

An Oilers field goal took that game into overtime, and it was filled with tension. Both teams knew that one mistake could cost them the game. The Bills won the coin toss and chose to receive the ball. They moved down the field quickly, setting up for a field goal. Steve Christie, the Bills' kicker, lined up for the kick. The stadium was silent. Everyone held their breath. Christie kicked the ball perfectly, sending it through the uprights. The Bills won 41-38. Their fans erupted in cheers. It was one of the greatest comebacks in NFL history.

The impact of this game was huge. For the Bills, it was a turning point. The win gave them the confidence to keep pushing forward. They went on to make four consecutive Super Bowl appearances. Although they didn't win a Super Bowl, their resilience and determination were inspiring. The Oilers, on the other hand, struggled after this game. The loss was hard to recover from. Over time, the team faced more challenges. Eventually, they moved to Tennessee and became the Titans.

The Greatest Comeback showed the power of never giving up. It taught fans and players alike that anything is possible in football. The game remains a legendary moment in NFL history. It reminds us that even when things look bleak, there's always a chance for a comeback. The Bills' incredible victory over the Oilers is a story of hope, determination, and the magic of football.

Football is filled with stories like these. Moments that capture our hearts and make us believe in the impossible. As we move forward, we'll explore more legendary games and unforgettable plays. Each story adds to the rich history of football, showing us why we love this game so much.

CHAPTER 6
THE CULTURE OF FOOTBALL

When I was a kid, one of my favorite memories was going to football games with my family. Before the game even started, we would set up our spot in the parking lot. We brought a grill, lots of food, and games to play. I didn't know it then, but this tradition is called tailgating. It's a big part of football culture. Tailgating is like a party before the game. It makes the whole day special, not just the game itself.

TAILGATING TRADITIONS

Tailgating has a long history. It started with college football games. The first college football game was between Rutgers and Princeton in 1869. Fans came early and brought food to share. They ate, talked, and got ready for the game together. This was the beginning of tailgating. The idea was simple: enjoy good food and good company before cheering on your team.

Today, tailgating is filled with fun activities. Barbecuing is a big part of it. People bring grills and cook their favorite foods. You'll see burgers, hot dogs, ribs, and chicken wings sizzling on the grill. The smell of the food fills the air and makes everyone hungry. Many people also bring side dishes like potato salad, baked beans, and chips. Some even have special recipes that they only make for game day.

Games are another big part of tailgating. Cornhole is a favorite. In this game, players toss beanbags at a raised plat-form with a hole in it. The goal is to get the beanbag through the hole. It sounds simple, but it's a lot of fun. Ladder toss is another popular game. Players throw bolas (two balls connected by a string) at a ladder-like structure. Each rung of the ladder has a different point value. These games add to the fun and excitement of tailgating. They also give people something to do while waiting for the game to start.

Some tailgaters take their setups to the next level. You might see custom tailgate trailers with TVs and sound systems. These trailers are like mini living rooms on wheels. They provide a comfortable place to watch pre-game shows and listen to music. Some fans even decorate their trailers with team colors and mascots. This makes their tailgate spot stand out and shows their team spirit. Themed tailgates are also popular. Fans decorate their area with team flags, banners, and tablecloths. They wear team jerseys and face paint. Sometimes, they even have team-themed food and drinks. These setups create a festive atmosphere and get everyone excited for the game.

Tailgating is not just about food and games. It's also about community. When you tailgate, you get to meet other fans. You share stories, laugh, and make new friends. Tailgating brings people together. It creates a sense of camaraderie and belonging. Some people have been tailgating with the same group for years. They look forward to seeing each other every football season. These friendships often last a lifetime.

Multi-generational tailgating traditions are common. Grandparents, parents, and kids all come together to celebrate. They pass down their tailgating traditions from one generation to the next. This keeps the tradition alive and makes it special for everyone. Tailgating becomes a family event that everyone looks forward to. It creates lasting memories and strengthens family bonds.

Tailgating Checklist

Here's a checklist to make sure you have everything you need for a great tailgate:

- **Grill:** Don't forget the charcoal or propane.
- **Food:** Bring burgers, hot dogs, ribs, chicken wings, and side dishes.
- **Drinks:** Pack plenty of water, soda, and juice.
- **Games:** Bring cornhole, ladder toss, or other fun games.
- **Chairs and Tables:** You'll need a place to sit and eat.
- **Cooler:** Keep your drinks and perishable food cold.
- **Team Gear:** Wear your team's colors and bring flags or banners.
- **Music:** A portable speaker can keep the energy high.
- **Trash Bags:** Clean up after yourself to keep the area nice.

Tailgating is a special part of football culture. It brings people together and makes game day even more fun. Whether you're grilling, playing games, or just hanging out with friends, tailgating adds to the excitement of football. So next time you go to a game, join the tailgating fun and create some great memories.

THE MOST FAMOUS FOOTBALL STADIUMS

Lambeau Field, home of the Green Bay Packers, is one of the most famous football stadiums in the world. Opened in 1957, it has hosted countless memorable games. The stadium is known for its "Frozen Tundra" reputation. This name comes from the cold weather games played there, especially during the winter months. Fans brave the freezing temperatures to cheer on their team. The history of Lambeau Field is rich with moments that have defined football. One of the most famous traditions here is the "Lambeau Leap." When a Packers player scores a touchdown, they sometimes leap into the stands to celebrate with the fans. This makes the connection between the players and fans even stronger.

Soldier Field in Chicago is another iconic stadium. It is the oldest stadium in the NFL in terms of original construction, opening in 1924. The stadium has undergone several renovations but still retains its historic charm. Soldier Field is home to the Chicago Bears. The stadium's name honors American soldiers, adding a layer of significance to every game played there. The blend of old and new design elements makes Soldier Field unique. The atmosphere is electric, especially when the Bears are playing well. Fans fill the stands, creating a sea of navy and orange. The stadium's history and connection to the military make it a special place for both football and its fans.

Arrowhead Stadium in Kansas City is known for being one of the loudest stadiums in the NFL. The home of the Kansas City Chiefs, Arrowhead was built in 1972. Fans here are famous for their enthusiasm and noise. In fact, the crowd roar at Arrowhead once reached an incredible 142.2 decibels, setting a record. This noise makes it tough for the opposing team to communicate and can give the Chiefs a big advantage. The stadium's design, with its steep stands, helps amplify the sound. When you're at Arrowhead, you can feel the energy and passion of the fans. They come in droves, wearing red and cheering loudly for their team.

AT&T Stadium, located in Arlington, Texas, is a state-of-the-art facility. Known as "Jerry World" after the Dallas Cowboys' owner Jerry Jones, it opened in 2009. The stadium features a massive retractable roof and one of the largest high-definition video boards in the world. This screen spans from one 20-yard line to the other, giving fans a perfect view of the action. AT&T Stadium can host over 100,000 fans, making it one of the largest stadiums in the NFL. The stadium's modern design and high-tech features make it a marvel. Fans enjoy a comfortable and immersive experience, complete with luxury suites and top-notch amenities.

MetLife Stadium in East Rutherford, New Jersey, is unique because it is the only NFL stadium shared by two teams. Both the New York Giants and New York Jets call MetLife home. The stadium opened in 2010 and can hold over 82,000 fans. The design allows for quick changes between Giants and Jets games, with team colors and logos switched out in a matter of hours. MetLife Stadium has hosted many significant events, including the Super Bowl. The atmosphere is always electric, with fans from both teams showing up in full force. Whether you're a Giants or Jets fan, MetLife offers a fantastic game day experience.

Ford Field in Detroit is a stadium known for its connection to the city's auto industry heritage. Opened in 2002, it is home to the Detroit Lions. The stadium features a unique design that incorporates an old warehouse, giving it a blend of modern and historical elements. Ford Field can hold over 65,000 fans and offers a comfortable and exciting environment. The stadium's location in downtown Detroit makes it easy for fans to attend games and enjoy the city's attractions. The connection to the auto industry is evident in the design and atmosphere, making Ford Field a special place for football fans.

Some college football stadiums are just as iconic. Michigan Stadium, known as "The Big House," is one of the most famous. Located in Ann Arbor, Michigan, it can hold over 100,000 fans. The sea of maize and blue creates an incredible atmosphere. Fans cheer loudly for the Michigan Wolverines, making every game an unforgettable experience. Tiger Stadium at LSU is another legendary venue. Known for its electrifying night games, the stadium comes alive under the lights. The fans, dressed in purple and gold, create a deafening roar that can be heard for miles. The energy and excitement at Tiger Stadium are unmatched.

These stadiums have become cultural landmarks. They host major events like Super Bowls and national championships, drawing fans from all over the country. The role of these stadiums in local economies is significant. They generate revenue from ticket sales, merchandise, and concessions. Local businesses benefit from the influx of fans, boosting the economy. The stadiums also create a sense of identity and pride for the communities. Fans feel a strong connection to their team and their stadium. This bond brings people together and fosters a sense of belonging.

Football stadiums are more than just places to watch games. They are places where memories are made, traditions are upheld, and communities come together. The atmosphere, history, and cultural significance of these stadiums make them special. Whether you're cheering for the Packers at Lambeau Field, the Bears at Soldier Field, or the Chiefs at

Arrowhead Stadium, the experience is unforgettable. Football stadiums are the heart of the game, and they play a big part in why we love football so much.

THE IMPACT OF FOOTBALL ON AMERICAN SOCIETY

Football has become a huge part of American culture. It's more than just a game; it's a tradition that brings people together. One of the best examples is Thanksgiving football games. Every year, families gather around the TV to watch football after enjoying their Thanksgiving meal. This tradition started in 1934 when the Detroit Lions played the Chicago Bears. Since then, it has become a beloved part of the holiday. Watching football on Thanksgiving is something that many families look forward to. It's a time to relax, cheer for your team, and enjoy being with family.

Another major event that shows football's importance is the Super Bowl. The Super Bowl is not just a football game; it's a national event. People who don't even watch football during the year tune in for the Super Bowl. It has become a day filled with parties, snacks, and excitement. The halftime show and commercials are just as famous as the game itself. Companies spend millions of dollars to create memorable ads because they know everyone will be watching. The Super Bowl brings people together and creates a sense of unity and celebration.

Football has a strong influence on media and entertainment. Many TV shows and movies are centered around football. These stories often show the hard work, teamwork, and challenges that players face. Movies like "Remember the Titans" and "Friday Night Lights" have become classics. They show how football can bring communities together and teach valuable life lessons. TV shows like "All American" also highlight the struggles and triumphs of high school football players. These stories resonate with people because they reflect the real-life experiences of many football players and fans.

Sports broadcasting has played a big role in popularizing football. When football games started being shown on TV, it allowed more people to watch and enjoy the sport. Networks like ESPN and FOX Sports provide in-depth coverage of games, player interviews, and expert analysis. This coverage keeps fans informed and engaged. Watching football on TV has become a favorite pastime for many people. The excitement of live games, combined with expert commentary, makes for an enjoyable viewing experience.

Football also has a significant economic impact. The sport generates a lot of money for local and national economies. Ticket sales for games bring in a lot of revenue. Fans buy tickets to watch their favorite teams play, filling stadiums with excited spectators. Merchandise sales also contribute to the economy. Fans love to buy jerseys, hats, and other items to show their support for their team. Broadcasting rights bring in even more money. Networks pay huge sums to air football games, knowing that millions of people will be watching.

Major events like the Super Bowl provide a huge economic boost. The host city sees an influx of visitors who spend money on hotels, restaurants, and other local businesses. This boost can have a lasting impact on the local economy. The Super Bowl also creates jobs, from construction workers building the stadium to vendors selling food and drinks. The economic benefits of football extend beyond the game itself, touching many aspects of the community.

Football's impact on American society is far-reaching. It

has become a tradition that brings people together, whether it's through Thanksgiving games or the Super Bowl. The sport's influence on media and entertainment keeps fans engaged and inspired. The economic contributions of football help support local and national economies. Football is more than just a sport; it's a powerful force that shapes American culture and identity.

FOOTBALL FANDOM: STORIES FROM THE STANDS

Football fans are some of the most dedicated and passionate people you will ever meet. They travel long distances to attend games, sometimes driving for hours or even flying across the country. Imagine a family from Texas who loves the Dallas Cowboys. They plan a trip to see their favorite team play in New York against the Giants. They pack their bags, wear their Cowboys jerseys, and make the journey just to cheer for their team in person. This dedication shows how much fans love football. They are willing to go the extra mile, literally, to support their team.

Fan loyalty is incredible. Some fans stick with their team through thick and thin, no matter how many games they win or lose. Take the Cleveland Browns, for example. The team has had many tough seasons, but their fans never give up on them. They show up to games, wear their Browns gear, and cheer loudly. This loyalty creates a strong bond between the team and its fans. It's about more than just winning; it's about being part of something bigger.

Unique traditions and rituals make being a football fan even more special. In Pittsburgh, Steelers fans have the "Terrible Towel." This bright yellow towel is waved in the air during games. It creates a sea of yellow in the stands and shows the team that the fans are behind them. The tradition started in 1975 and has become a symbol of Steelers pride. Another great example is the "12th Man" tradition of the Seattle Seahawks. The fans are so loud and supportive that they are considered the extra player on the field, the "12th Man." Seahawks fans even raise a special flag before each game to honor their role. These rituals make the game day experience unique and memorable.

Fan communities and clubs help fans connect with each other. Fan clubs often organize meetups and events, allowing fans to share their love for the team. Online communities are also popular. Fans can join forums, social media groups, and websites dedicated to their team. They discuss games, share news, and even make new friends. Tailgate groups, which were discussed earlier, are another way fans come together. These groups meet before games to eat, play games, and get excited for the match. The sense of community makes being a football fan even more enjoyable.

Personal stories from fans add a special touch to the football experience. One fan, Sarah, recalls her first game at Lambeau Field. She went with her dad, who had been a Packers fan his whole life. They wore matching jerseys and cheered together. The Packers won, and Sarah even got an autograph from her favorite player. This memory is something she will cherish forever. Another fan, Mike, tells a story about a game where he got to meet the team. He was part of a special event and got to shake hands with the players. Mike says it was a dream come true and made him an even bigger fan.

Family traditions centered around football are common. Many families gather every Sunday to watch the game together. They cook special game day snacks and wear their team colors. This time together strengthens family bonds and creates lasting memories. One family, the Johnsons, have a tradition of playing a game of touch football in their backyard before watching the big game. It's a way to have fun and get into the football spirit. These traditions make football more than just a sport; they make it a part of family life.

The passion of football fans is unmatched. They travel long distances, stay loyal through tough times, and create unique traditions. Fan communities and clubs help them connect, and personal stories add a special touch. Family traditions centered around football bring everyone closer together. The dedication and love of football fans make the sport even more special.

Football fans are the heart and soul of the sport. Their passion, loyalty, and dedication create a vibrant and exciting atmosphere. Whether it's through unique traditions, fan communities, or personal stories, fans make football more than just a game. Their love for the sport brings people together and creates lasting memories. As we move forward, let's keep exploring the incredible world of football and the amazing people who make it so special.

———

CHAPTER 7
INSPIRATIONAL STORIES OF PERSEVERANCE

love hearing stories about people who never gave up. One story that always stood out to me was that of Rudy Ruettiger. Imagine being a kid who dreams big but faces many challenges. Rudy's story shows how determination and hard work can turn dreams into reality.

THE STORY OF RUDY RUETTIGER: FROM WALK-ON TO LEGEND

Rudy Ruettiger grew up in Joliet, Illinois. He was the third of 14 children in a working-class family. Life wasn't easy for Rudy. His family didn't have a lot of money, and he had to work hard from a young age. Rudy also struggled in school because he had dyslexia, a learning disability that made reading and writing difficult. Despite these challenges, Rudy had a big dream. He wanted to play football for Notre Dame, one of the most famous college football teams. This dream seemed impossible because Rudy was small for a football player, standing only 5'6" and weighing 165 pounds.

Rudy's journey to Notre Dame was tough. After high school, he didn't have the grades to get into college. So, he enlisted in the Navy and served two tours during the Vietnam War. When he returned, he worked in a power plant to save money for college. Rudy applied to Notre Dame several times but was rejected because of his grades. He didn't give up. Rudy enrolled at Holy Cross College, a junior college near Notre Dame. He worked hard to improve his grades, studying late into the night. After three rejections, Rudy was finally accepted to Notre Dame in 1974. His dream was one step closer to becoming true.

At Notre Dame, Rudy faced more challenges. He joined the football team as a walk-on player, which means he wasn't given a scholarship. Walk-ons often don't get to play in games. They help the varsity team practice. Rudy trained hard every day. He pushed himself to the limit, showing his teammates and coaches that he had heart. His determination earned him their respect and support. Rudy's hard work paid off in his final game against Georgia Tech in 1975. Coach Dan Devine decided to let Rudy play in the last moments of the game. Rudy sacked the quarterback, and the crowd went wild. His teammates lifted him onto their shoulders and carried him off the field. It was the first time in Notre Dame history that a player was carried off the field by his teammates.

Rudy's story didn't end there. His incredible journey was turned into a movie called "Rudy," which has inspired many people. Rudy became a motivational speaker, sharing his story with others. He shows us that even when things seem impossible, hard work and determination can make dreams come true. Rudy's legacy lives on, reminding us that we can achieve great things if we never give up.

THE UNDERDOG STORY OF KURT WARNER

Kurt Warner grew up in Iowa, where he loved playing football. He played college football at the University of Northern Iowa. Despite his talent, he faced many setbacks. After college, he went undrafted, which means no NFL team picked him. This was a huge disappointment. To support his family, Kurt worked at a grocery store, earning just $5.50 an hour. He stocked shelves and checked out customers, but he never gave up on his dream. He kept working out and practicing, hoping for another chance to play football.

Kurt's next step was the Arena Football League. He joined the Iowa Barnstormers and quickly became a star. The Arena League is different from the NFL. The field is smaller, and the game is faster. Kurt's quick thinking and strong arm helped him excel. He led his team to two Arena Bowl appearances. His success caught the attention of NFL scouts. Kurt then played for the Amsterdam Admirals in NFL Europe. He continued to impress with his skills and determination. These experiences prepared him for the next big opportunity.

Kurt's big break came with the St. Louis Rams. In 1999, the Rams' starting quarterback, Trent Green, got injured. Kurt stepped in as the starter. No one expected much from him, but he shocked everyone. He led the Rams to victory in Super Bowl XXXIV and was named the Super Bowl MVP. That season, he also won the NFL MVP award. He repeated this achievement in 2001. Kurt's incredible rise from grocery store worker to NFL star was a story of perseverance and hard work. He showed that you should never give up, no matter how tough things get.

Kurt Warner's legacy goes beyond his football achievements. He was inducted into the Pro Football Hall of Fame, which is a huge honor. Kurt also became a motivational speaker and philanthropist. He shares his story with others, inspiring them to chase their dreams. He started the First Things First Foundation to help those in need. Kurt's journey from humble beginnings to NFL stardom shows that anything is possible with hard work and determination. His story continues to inspire people around the world.

OVERCOMING ADVERSITY: THE STORY OF ALEX SMITH

Alex Smith's early career was full of promise. In 2005, the San Francisco 49ers drafted him first overall. That's a big deal. Being the first pick means teams think you are the best player available. Alex worked hard and showed his talent. By 2011, he had led the 49ers to the NFC Championship Game. The team was just one win away from the Super Bowl. Alex was praised for his leadership and skill. He had a bright future ahead of him. Little did he know that his biggest challenge was yet to come.

In 2018, Alex faced a life-changing moment. During a game, he suffered a severe leg injury. It was a compound fracture, meaning the bone broke through the skin. The injury was gruesome and painful. Doctors rushed him to surgery to fix his leg. But things got worse. He developed a life-threatening infection. The infection was so bad that doctors considered amputating his leg. Alex and his family were frightened. They didn't know if he would ever walk again, let alone play football. Multiple surgeries followed. Each one aimed to save his leg and his life.

Alex's recovery was long and tough. He spent months in the hospital. His leg was in a brace, and he couldn't move it.

Rehabilitation was painful and slow. But Alex never gave up. He worked tirelessly to regain his strength. His family supported him every step of the way. After many months of hard work, he made an incredible comeback. In 2020, he returned to play for the Washington Football Team. Fans and players were amazed. His determination and bravery were inspiring. Alex's efforts paid off when he was named the NFL Comeback Player of the Year.

Alex Smith's story is more than just a football tale. It's a lesson in resilience and hope. He showed that even when things seem impossible, you can overcome them. Alex became a symbol of strength for many people. Other athletes and individuals facing tough times looked up to him. He also started advocating for injury awareness and recovery. Alex wanted to help others who faced similar struggles. His journey is a reminder that with courage and hard work, you can achieve great things.

THE COMEBACK OF PEYTON MANNING

Peyton Manning started his NFL career with a bang. Being drafted first overall in the 1998 NFL Draft by the Indianapolis Colts was just the beginning. He quickly showed everyone why he deserved that top spot. Peyton led the Colts to many victories, including a Super Bowl XLI win. He earned multiple MVP awards for his outstanding performances. Peyton's ability to read defenses and make quick decisions made him one of the best quarterbacks. His time with the Colts was filled with record-breaking achievements and unforgettable moments. Fans admired his dedication and skill, making him a beloved figure in football.

But Peyton's career hit a major roadblock. He suffered a

severe neck injury that required multiple surgeries. The surgeries were risky, and Peyton had to miss the entire 2011 season to recover. The Colts, worried about his health, made a tough decision. They released him, letting go of one of the greatest quarterbacks in their history. Peyton faced uncertainty about his future. Many wondered if he would ever play again. The injury was not just a physical challenge but an emotional one too. Peyton had to prove to himself and others that he could return to the field.

Peyton's comeback story is nothing short of amazing. He signed with the Denver Broncos and quickly returned to elite form. In 2013, he broke the single-season touchdown record, showing everyone he was still a top player. His leadership and skill led the Broncos to many wins. The highlight of his comeback was leading the Broncos to victory in Super Bowl 50. Peyton's determination and hard work paid off. He showed that even after a major setback, it's possible to achieve great things. His story is a testament to resilience and perseverance.

Peyton Manning's impact on football goes beyond his stats. He became a mentor to many young players, sharing his knowledge and experience. His dedication to the game and his teammates earned him respect from everyone. Peyton's influence is seen in how the game is played today. He set a standard for preparation and excellence that many strive to follow. His legacy as one of the greatest quarterbacks will always be remembered.

TEAMWORK MAKES THE DREAM WORK: THE 2007 NEW YORK GIANTS

The 2007 NFL season was full of excitement and surprises. The New England Patriots were on a mission to make history. They had won all 16 of their regular season games, a perfect record. No team had ever finished a season 19-0, and the Patriots were determined to be the first. Led by quarterback Tom Brady and coach Bill Belichick, the Patriots were a powerhouse. They had star players like Randy Moss, who caught many of Brady's touchdown passes. The Patriots seemed unstoppable, and fans expected them to win the Super Bowl easily.

On the other hand, the New York Giants were seen as underdogs. They faced many ups and downs. During the regular season, the team struggled with consistency. Some games they played well, while in others, they couldn't find their rhythm. Injuries also hit the team hard. Key players went down, making it even tougher to win games. Despite these challenges, the team never gave up. They kept fighting, determined to turn their season around and they managed to make it to the playoffs.

The Giants' playoff journey was nothing short of remarkable. They entered the playoffs as underdogs. In the first round, they upset the higher-seeded Dallas Cowboys. The Cowboys had beaten them twice in the regular season, but the Giants played with grit and determination. Next, they faced the Green Bay Packers in the NFC Championship Game. The game was in freezing conditions at Lambeau Field, but the Giants didn't let the cold affect them. They played a tough game and won in overtime, securing their spot in the Super Bowl.

The Super Bowl started with both teams playing strong defense. The game was close, with neither team able to pull away. The Patriots scored first, but the Giants quickly answered with a field goal. As the game went on, it became clear that this would be a battle until the end. Then came one of the most memorable plays in Super Bowl history. With just over a minute left in the game, the Giants were down 14-10. Eli Manning took the snap and found himself under heavy pressure. He dodged several defenders and threw a high pass down the field. David Tyree jumped up, caught the ball against his helmet, and held on as he fell to the ground. This incredible "helmet catch" kept the Giants' hopes alive.

With the clock ticking down, Manning led the Giants down the field. They reached the Patriots' 13-yard line. Manning then threw a perfect pass to Plaxico Burress in the corner of the end zone. Burress caught the ball for a touchdown, giving the Giants a 17-14 lead. The Giants' defense then took over, putting immense pressure on Tom Brady. They sacked him several times, preventing the Patriots from making a comeback. The Giants had done the unthinkable. They defeated the Patriots, ending their quest for a perfect season.

Eli Manning's performance was outstanding. He showed great leadership and made clutch plays when it mattered most. His calmness under pressure was key to the Giants' victory. David Tyree's helmet catch became an iconic moment in Super Bowl history. Plaxico Burress's game-winning touchdown sealed the deal. The Giants' defense, led by players like Michael Strahan and Justin Tuck, played a crucial role. They pressured Tom Brady and disrupted the Patriots' offense.

The aftermath of this game was huge. The Patriots' dream of a perfect season was shattered. Fans and players were heartbroken, but they knew they had witnessed an incredible game. For the Giants, this victory cemented their place in Super Bowl history. They became known as the giant-slayers, the team that took down the mighty Patriots. This game is still remembered as one of the greatest upsets in sports history.

The end of the Patriots' perfect season had a lasting impact on the NFL. It showed that no team is unbeatable, no matter how strong they are. The Giants' victory inspired other underdog teams to believe in themselves. It reminded everyone that hard work, determination, and belief can lead to incredible outcomes. The legacy of Super Bowl XLII continues to inspire players and fans alike.

INSPIRATIONAL STORIES FROM YOUTH AND HIGH SCHOOL FOOTBALL

Imagine playing football with boys and being the fastest one on the field. That's what Sam Gordon did. Sam was a young girl who loved football. She joined a boys' league and quickly became a star. Her speed and skill were amazing. She could outrun almost anyone. Sam broke tackles and scored touchdowns, proving that girls can compete with boys. Her story inspired many young girls to follow their dreams, showing them that they could play football too. Sam's success on the field sent a powerful message about breaking barriers and believing in yourself.

Then there's Jake Olson. Jake loved football, but he faced a huge challenge. He lost his sight when he was just 12 years old. Most people would think playing football was impossible for him. But not Jake. He didn't let his blindness stop him. Jake worked hard and became a long snapper for the USC

Trojans. This position requires precise snaps of the football during punts and field goals. Jake practiced tirelessly with his teammates and coaches. He learned to snap the ball by feeling his surroundings and trusting his instincts. His determination and hard work paid off when he played in a game for USC. Jake's story is a testament to the power of perseverance and the human spirit.

Teamwork and community support are crucial in youth football. Coaches and mentors play a big role in guiding young players. They teach them the skills they need and help them grow as athletes and people. Community support is also important. When the whole community cheers for young players, it boosts their confidence. It shows them they are part of something bigger. This support helps them develop their talents and achieve their goals. The encouragement from family, friends, and neighbors can make all the difference.

These stories teach us valuable lessons. Sam Gordon and Jake Olson show us that with hard work and determination, we can overcome any challenge. They remind us of the importance of perseverance and resilience. When we face obstacles, we should keep pushing forward. Teamwork and supporting each other are also key. No one achieves greatness alone. Working together and helping our teammates makes us stronger.

You can take these lessons and apply them to your own life. Set personal goals and work hard to achieve them. Support your friends and build positive relationships. Remember, you can overcome any challenge with determination and resilience.

CHAPTER 8
FOOTBALL TRIVIA AND FUN FACTS

M y nephew is a football fanatic, and he and his friends love testing each other with football trivia. They spend hours quizzing each other on everything from famous players to unforgettable games. These trivia sessions have turned into a fun way to learn more about football. This chapter is filled with trivia questions that will challenge your knowledge and teach you some cool facts about football history.

TRIVIA QUESTIONS ABOUT FOOTBALL HISTORY

Let's start with some questions to get your brain working. These questions and interesting facts cover important events and milestones in football history. See how many you can answer correctly!

———

First, let's go back to the very first Super Bowl. In what year was the first Super Bowl played? The answer is 1967.

—————

Do you know which team won the first Super Bowl? Was it the Green Bay Packers, Kansas City Chiefs, New York Jets, or Dallas Cowboys? If you guessed the Green Bay Packers, you're right! The Packers won the game 35-10 against the Kansas City Chiefs. This game marked the beginning of what would become one of the biggest sports events in the world.

—————

Here's another question for you: True or False: The NFL was founded in 1920. If you said true, great job! The NFL was indeed founded in 1920.

—————

What was the original name of the NFL? It was originally called the American Professional Football Association (APFA). The league changed its name to the National Football League (NFL) in 1922. This change helped solidify the league's identity and set it on the path to becoming the premier football league in the United States (refer to Chapter 1).

—————

Here's a question to challenge you: Which team played in the NFL from 1929 until 1932? Was it the Staten Island Stapletons,

Brooklyn Dodgers, Portsmouth Spartans, or Akron Pros? The correct answer is the Staten Island Stapleton. This team may not be well-known today, but they played a role in shaping the early years of the NFL.

––––––––

Who was the first African American professional football player in the USA? Was it Charles W. Follis, Fritz Pollard, Kenny Washington, or Joe Lillard? The correct answer is Charles W. Follis. His contributions to the sport paved the way for future generations of African American players.

––––––––

Who invented the forward pass? John Heisman (yes, that Heisman - like the trophy!) is credited with introducing innovations like the forward pass and the use of the scoreboard.

––––––––

When was the first football game played? That's right! We talked about it in Chapter 1 - if you said November 6, 1869, you are right!

––––––––

Who played in the first football game? Princeton and Rutgers.

––––––––

The Super Bowl is famous for being the most-watched event on TV, but it's also the second biggest day for food consumption in the United States, right behind Thanksgiving.

Do you know why the quarterback is called a quarterback? In early football formations, players were positioned based on their distance from the line of scrimmage. The player closest was the fullback, and the player behind him was the halfback. The "quarterback" stood even closer, a quarter of the way back.

Helmets weren't always required. Football helmets weren't mandatory until 1943!

————

The longest football game ever played (to date) was in 1971 between the Miami Dolphins and Kansas City Chiefs, lasting a whopping 82 minutes and 40 seconds due to overtime.

————

The longest field goal in NFL history (to date) is 66 yards, made by Justin Tucker of the Baltimore Ravens in 2021. Before this, the record was held by Matt Prater of the Denver Broncos at 64 yards in 2013. Finally, prior to Prater, the record was held by Tom Dempsey who famously kicked a 63 yard field goal for the New Orleans Saints in 1970. Dempsey's kick was particularly notable because he did it with a modified shoe, as he was born without toes on his right foot. Several other kickers matched Dempsey's record before Prate broke it in 2013.

————

What year was the first NFL draft? 1936

————

Who was the heaviest NFL player (to date)? Aaron Gibson, an offensive tackle who weighed 410 pounds during his career. He played for multiple teams from 1999 to 2006.

————

Oldest NFL Player: The oldest player to ever play in the NFL (to date) was George Blanda, who retired at the age of 48 in 1975. Blanda played 26 seasons as a quarterback and kicker, setting records for both longevity and scoring.

———

Why are footballs called "pigskins?" Early versions of footballs were made from pig bladders, which is why the ball is often referred to as a "pigskin". Modern footballs are now made of leather, but the nickname has stuck.

———

While most major sports try to avoid playing games on Christmas, the NFL has games on December 25. The first occurred in 1971, and the most famous Christmas Day game is known as the "Christmas Day Miracle," where the Miami Dolphins beat the Kansas City Chiefs in double overtime during the playoffs.

———

The Highest Scoring Game in NFL History (to date): The highest-scoring game in NFL history occurred in 1966, when the Washington Redskins defeated the New York Giants with a total score of 72-41. That's a combined total of 113 points!

———

Who was the first female NFL coach? Jen Welter became the first female coach in the NFL when she was hired by the

Arizona Cardinals as an assistant coaching intern for training camp and the preseason in 2015.

————

What is the oldest stadium in the NFL today? You got it - we talked about it in Chapter 6. Soldier Field in Chicago is the older stadium still in use by the NFL, as of 2024. It opened in 1924.

————

In what year was the instant replay introduced in the NFL? The first instant replay system was developed in 1986.

————

Football players in the military: some famous NFL players also served in the U.S. military. Notably, Pat Tillman left the Arizona Cardinals to join the Army after the 9/11 attacks, sacrificing his football career. He tragically died in Afghanistan in 2004.

————

Most Super Bowl Wins - As of 2024, the teams with the most Super Bowl victories are the Pittsburgh Steelers and the New England Patriots, each with six championships.

————

Longest NFL Streak Without a Playoff Win - As of 2023, the Detroit Lions hold the record for the longest playoff victory drought. Before 2023, they hadn't won a playoff game since 1991, despite being one of the oldest teams in the league.

———

Longest Winning Streak in College Football - As of 2023, Oklahoma holds the record for the longest winning streak in college football history with 47 consecutive wins from 1953 to 1957.

———

Most National Champions - As of 2023, Alabama holds the record for the most national championships with 18.

———

The Minnesota Golden Gophers football team holds the distinction of winning three consecutive national championships in 1934 to 1936.

———

As of 2024, no NFL has won three Super Bowls in a row. Eight teams have won back-to-back Super Bowls: the Packers (1966 and 1967), Dolphins (1972 and 1973), Steelers (1974 and 1975, as well as 1978 and 1980), 49ers (1988 and 1989), Cowboys (1992 and 1993), Broncos (1997 and 1998), Patriots (2003 and 2004), and the Chiefs (2023 and 2024).

———

What is the longest touchdown pass in NFL history to date? 99 yards! This feat has been accomplished 13 times, with the first occurring in 1939 and the most recent in 2011.

———

Similarly, what is the longest touchdown run in NFL history to date? It was also 99 yards - but - this feat has only been accomplished once, to date, in 1983 by Tony Dorsett of the Dallas Cowboys.

———

Who is the winning-est coach in NFL history to date? The answer is Don Shula (Dolphins and Colts), who holds the record for the most career wins as a head coach with 347 total victories (including both regular season and postseason wins). Number 2 is Bill Belichick (Patriots and Browns) at 331 and number 3 is Georg Halas (Bears).

———

How many coaches have never had a losing season an as NFL head coach? The answer is three: Marty Schottenheimer (Browns, Chiefs, Redskins/Washington Football Team, Chargers), in a 21-year career, never had fewer than 7 wins (but had some seasons with a record of 7 and 7); John Madden (Raiders) in a 10-year career never had a losing season; and Mike Tomlin (Steelers) has never had a losing season during his tenure, which began in 2007. Entering the

2024 - 2025 season, Tomlin has a whopping 17 winning seasons, and he's still coaching!

———

Learning about football history through trivia is a fun way to deepen your knowledge of the game. Each question and answer reveals a piece of the puzzle that makes up the rich history of football. Now, let's dive into these questions and see how much you know about the game you love!

FUN FACTS ABOUT NFL TEAMS

Did you know that the Green Bay Packers are the only team in the NFL owned by their fans? This makes them unique among professional sports teams. The Packers are based in a small city, but their community ownership gives fans a special bond with the team. Every few years, the Packers sell shares to raise money for improvements. These shares don't pay dividends or appreciate in value, but they give fans a sense of pride and ownership. Imagine having your name listed as a part-owner of an NFL team. It's a cool way to show your support and love for the Packers.

The Pittsburgh Steelers are known for their winning ways. They are tied for the most Super Bowl wins, with six championships to their name. The Steelers' success started in the 1970s when they won four Super Bowls in six years. This period is often called the "Steel Curtain" era because of their dominant defense. The team continued to win in the 2000s, adding two more Super Bowls. Fans of the Steelers are proud of their team's achievements and look forward to adding more trophies to their collection. The Steelers' history of winning makes them one of the most respected teams in the NFL. And don't forget those "Terrible Towels" we talked about earlier! Fans wave these yellow towels during games to show their support and create a sea of yellow in the stands. The tradition started in 1975 when the team's radio broad-caster, Myron Cope, encouraged fans to bring yellow towels to a playoff game. The idea was a hit, and the Terrible Towel became a symbol of Steelers pride. Today, fans bring their Terrible Towels to every game, waving them with enthusiasm and creating an electric atmosphere in the stadium.

The New England Patriots hold the record for the most consecutive playoff appearances. They made the playoffs 11 years in a row, from 2009 to 2019. This streak is a testament to their consistency and excellence. Led by coach Bill Belichick and quarterback Tom Brady, the Patriots won multiple Super Bowls during this period (and are tied with the Steelers at six total Super Bowl wins). Their success was built on hard work, smart strategy, and teamwork. Fans of the Patriots enjoyed watching their team compete at the highest level year after year. The Patriots' record shows that dedication and effort can lead to sustained success.

One of the most remarkable achievements in NFL history is the Miami Dolphins' perfect season in 1972. The Dolphins won all 14 regular-season games and then went on to win the Super Bowl. No other team has ever finished a season unde-feated and won the championship. This incredible feat made the Dolphins a legendary team. Fans still celebrate the 1972 season as a symbol of perfection. The Dolphins' perfect season is a reminder that anything is possible with hard work and determination.

The Green Bay Packers have a fun tradition known as the "Lambeau Leap." After scoring a touchdown, Packers players

often jump into the stands to celebrate with fans. This tradition started in 1993 when LeRoy Butler leaped into the crowd
after recovering a fumble and scoring a touchdown. The fans
loved it, and the Lambeau Leap became a regular part of
Packers games. It shows the close connection between the
players and their supporters. The Lambeau Leap is a special
moment that makes every touchdown even more exciting for
fans at Lambeau Field.

RECORD-BREAKING MOMENTS IN FOOTBALL

Have you ever wondered who holds the record for the most
career receiving yards in NFL history? It's Jerry Rice, and his
record is truly amazing. Jerry Rice racked up 22,895 receiving
yards over his career. This record shows his incredible skill
and consistency. Imagine catching passes game after game,
year after year, and still being the best. Jerry Rice played for
several teams, but he is best known for his time with the San
Francisco 49ers. His dedication and hard work set him apart
from other receivers. Every young player dreams of breaking
his record, but it's a tough one to beat.

Another incredible record belongs to Emmitt Smith. He
holds the record for the most career rushing yards. Emmitt
ran for 18,355 yards during his time in the NFL. He played
most of his career with the Dallas Cowboys. Emmitt's ability
to find gaps in the defense and break through tackles made
him a legend. He wasn't the biggest or the fastest, but his
determination and vision on the field were unmatched.
Emmitt's record shows that with hard work and persistence,
you can achieve great things. It's a record that will be remembered for a long time.

Teams also have some amazing records. For example, the

Chicago Bears have the most Hall of Famers. This means more Bears players have been recognized for their greatness than players from any other team. The Bears have a rich history full of legendary players like Walter Payton, Mike Ditka, and Dick Butkus. Each of these players made a huge impact on the game. Being inducted into the Hall of Fame is one of the highest honors in football, and the Bears having the most inductees shows their long history of excellence and contributions to the sport.

The San Francisco 49ers hold the record for the most consecutive road wins. They won 18 road games in a row from 1988 to 1990. Winning on the road is tough because you're playing in front of the other team's fans, but the 49ers managed to do it consistently. This record highlights the strength and focus of the team during those years. With players like Joe Montana and Jerry Rice leading the way, the 49ers were nearly unstoppable. Their ability to win no matter where they played is a testament to their skill and determination.

Some records are set in a single game. Adrian Peterson set the record for the most rushing yards in a single game when he ran for 296 yards in 2007. This incredible performance took place when he was playing for the Minnesota Vikings against the San Diego Chargers. Adrian's speed, strength, and agility were on full display that day. Breaking tackles and outrunning defenders, he showed why he was one of the best running backs in the league. This record-breaking game is still talked about as one of the greatest performances in NFL history.

On September 28, 1951, Norm Van Brocklin set an NFL record that still stands today, throwing for an astounding 554 yards in a single game. Playing for the Los Angeles Rams,

Van Brocklin led his team to a dominant 54-14 victory over the New York Yanks. This historic performance came in just the second game of the 1951 season, and Van Brocklin was in top form, completing 27 of 41 passes with five touchdowns. At the time, the NFL was more reliant on the running game, making Van Brocklin's feat even more remarkable. His ability to connect with multiple receivers, especially Hall of Famer Elroy "Crazylegs" Hirsch, who accounted for 173 yards and four touchdowns, was a key factor in the record-setting performance. Van Brocklin's precision and vision on the field helped him achieve a mark that many believed would never be reached in an era where passing wasn't as emphasized as it is today. Despite the evolution of the game and the rise of many prolific passers in modern football, Van Brocklin's record remains unmatched. Quarterbacks have come close, but his 554-yard single-game total still stands as one of the most impressive individual achievements in NFL history, a testament to his exceptional talent and place among the greats.

Another amazing record is the fastest touchdown in Super Bowl history. Devin Hester returned the opening kickoff for a touchdown in just 14 seconds during Super Bowl XLI. He played for the Chicago Bears, and his speed and agility left everyone in awe. As soon as he caught the ball, he took off, weaving through defenders and racing down the field. The crowd went wild, and it was a thrilling start to the game. This record-breaking moment shows how exciting football can be and how quickly the game can change.

FAMOUS FOOTBALL QUOTES

Football has given us some of the most inspiring words from players and coaches. These quotes can motivate you and make you feel part of something big. One of the most famous quotes comes from Vince Lombardi. He once said, "Winning isn't everything, it's the only thing." Lombardi was the head coach of the Green Bay Packers. He led the team to five NFL Championships, including the first two Super Bowls. This quote shows his strong belief in the importance of winning. For Lombardi, winning meant hard work, discipline, and dedication.

Another great quote comes from Jerry Rice, a legendary wide receiver. He said, "Today I will do what others won't, so tomorrow I can accomplish what others can't." Rice's words remind us that hard work and sacrifice lead to success. He played most of his career with the San Francisco 49ers and set many records. His dedication to practice and fitness made him one of the greatest players ever. This quote encourages you to put in the extra effort now to achieve your dreams later.

John Madden, a famous coach and commentator, gave us a funny but true quote. He said, "The road to Easy Street goes through the sewer." Madden's quote means that success often comes after hard times. He coached the Oakland Raiders to a Super Bowl victory and later became a well-loved commentator. His colorful personality and deep knowledge of the game made him a fan favorite. Madden's quote teaches us that we must face challenges to reach our goals.

Yogi Berra, known for his funny and clever sayings, once said, "Football is 90% mental and the other half is physical." This quote makes us smile because the math doesn't add up, but it also tells a deeper truth. Berra was a baseball player but often commented on other sports. His words remind us that having the right mindset is just as important as physical ski'l in football. The quote shows that thinking smart and staying focused can make a big difference in the game.

Joe Namath made a bold prediction before Super Bowl III. He said, "We're going to win the game. I guarantee it." Namath played for the New York Jets, and his team was the underdog against the Baltimore Colts. Despite the odds, Namath's confidence inspired his teammates. The Jets won the game 16-7, and Namath's guarantee became one of the most famous moments in football history. His words show the power of belief and self-confidence.

These quotes from football legends and moments capture the spirit of the game. They inspire us to work hard, face challenges, and believe in ourselves. Whether you're on the field or cheering from the stands, these words remind us why we love football.

BIZARRE FOOTBALL MOMENTS

Football is full of moments that leave fans scratching their heads or laughing out loud. Some plays and events are so unusual that they become legendary. One such moment is known as the "Butt Fumble" by Mark Sanchez. In 2012, during a game between the New York Jets and the New England Patriots, Sanchez tried to run the ball but collided with his teammate's rear end. The ball popped loose, and the Patriots recovered it, scoring a touchdown. This bizarre play became famous for its oddity and is still talked about today. It shows that in football, anything can happen.

Another strange event in football history is the "Snow

Plow Game." This game took place in 1982 between the Miami Dolphins and the New England Patriots. The field was covered in snow, making it hard for players to move and see. Late in the game, a snowplow operator cleared a spot on the field for the Patriots' kicker, allowing him to make a successful field goal. The Patriots won the game 3-0, but the use of the snowplow sparked controversy. This moment is remembered for its unusual and unexpected twist, showing how weather can play a big role in football.

Football has also seen some strange and unusual events that are hard to believe. One of these is the "Fog Bowl" between the Chicago Bears and the Philadelphia Eagles in 1988. A thick fog rolled in during the game, making it almost impossible for players and fans to see. Despite the poor visibility, the game continued, and the Bears won 20-12. The Fog Bowl is remembered for the eerie atmosphere and the challenges it presented to both teams. It's a reminder that sometimes, nature can change the game in surprising ways.

Another unusual event was the blackout during Super Bowl XLVII between the Baltimore Ravens and the San Francisco 49ers. The game was going smoothly when suddenly, the lights went out in the stadium. The blackout lasted for 34 minutes, causing confusion and a delay. Players tried to stay loose, and fans waited patiently for the game to resume. When the lights finally came back on, the 49ers made a strong comeback, but the Ravens held on to win. The blackout added an unexpected twist to an already exciting game, making it a memorable moment in Super Bowl history.

Football games sometimes have quirky and funny moments that make fans laugh. One such moment happened during a Monday Night Football game when a cat ran onto the field. The small black cat darted around, avoiding players and officials. The game had to be paused while the cat was chased off the field. Fans cheered and laughed at the unexpected visitor, and the moment became an internet sensation. It shows that even in a serious game, funny things can happen that make everyone smile.

Another famous quirky moment is the "Heidi Game." In 1968, a game between the New York Jets and the Oakland Raiders was cut off by NBC to show the movie "Heidi." The Jets were leading when the broadcast switched, but the Raiders scored two touchdowns in the final minute to win the game. Fans were furious that they missed the exciting finish. This incident led to changes in how networks handle game broadcasts, ensuring that games are shown in their entirety. The Heidi Game is a funny reminder of how important football is to fans.

Sometimes, unlikely heroes emerge in football, surprising everyone with their performances. One such hero was backup quarterback Nick Foles. In the 2017 season, Foles stepped in for the injured Carson Wentz and led the Philadelphia Eagles to their first Super Bowl victory. Foles played brilliantly, even catching a touchdown pass in a play called the "Philly Special." His unexpected rise to glory made him a hero in Philadelphia and an inspiration to players everywhere. It shows that anyone can step up and make a difference when given the chance.

Football is full of bizarre and unexpected moments that make the game even more exciting. These strange plays, unusual events, and quirky moments add to the rich tapestry of football history. They remind us that anything can happen on the field, and sometimes, the most unexpected moments are the ones we remember the most.

———

CHAPTER 9
THE FUTURE OF FOOTBALL

Whan I first saw a women's football game, I was amazed. The players were fierce, fast, and skilled. They tackled hard, made incredible catches, and showed great teamwork. It is clear that women's football was growing, and I wanted to learn more about it.

THE RISE OF WOMEN'S FOOTBALL LEAGUES

Women's football has come a long way. More and more people are watching and playing the game. One big reason for this is the Women's Football Alliance (WFA). The WFA is a professional women's tackle football league. It started small but has grown a lot. Today, the WFA National Championship Games are played at the Hall of Fame in Canton, Ohio. These games are even shown live on ESPN2 and the Women's Sports Network. This helps more people see and appreciate the talent in women's football.

International competitions are also helping women's football grow. Women's World Cup events are becoming more popular. Teams from different countries compete, showing that football is loved all around the world. These events give female athletes a chance to shine on a big stage. They inspire young girls everywhere to dream big and play football.

Many female players have made a big impact on the game. One standout player is Sam Gordon, who we discussed earlier. She became famous as a youth football sensation. When she was just nine years old, a video of her playing went viral. She was fast, strong, and fearless. Her skills on the field showed that girls can be just as good as boys at football. Sam's story has inspired many young girls to play the game.

Katie Sowers is another trailblazer. She made history as the first woman to coach in a Super Bowl. She was an offensive assistant coach for the San Francisco 49ers. Katie's journey to the NFL was not easy. She faced many challenges, including being denied a coaching position because of her sexual orientation. But she didn't give up. She played in the Women's Football Alliance for eight years and worked hard to become a coach. Her success shows that with hard work and determination, anything is possible.

Despite these successes, female players still face challenges. One big challenge is gender bias. This means people might think less of female players just because they are women. This can make it harder for them to get support and funding. Men's leagues often get more money and attention. This makes it difficult for women's leagues to grow.

However, things are starting to change. Women's football is getting more visibility. More people are watching games and supporting female players. Mainstream media is also helping. When networks like ESPN show women's football games, it brings more attention to the sport. Sponsors are starting to notice too. They are supporting women's football more, which helps the leagues grow.

The future of women's football looks bright. As more people see and support the game, it will continue to grow. We can hope for more professional leagues and bigger international competitions. Young girls will have more opportunities to play and succeed in football.

FEMALE COACHES IN THE NFL

When you think about football coaches, you might picture men in caps and headsets, shouting plays from the sideline. But today, women are breaking into this world and making a big impact. Jen Welter and Katie Sowers are two trailblazers who have shown that women can coach at the highest levels of football.

Jen Welter made history as the first female coach in the NFL. She joined the Arizona Cardinals as an assistant coaching intern. Before that, she played football herself, even in men's leagues. Imagine trying to earn respect in a field where people think you don't belong. Jen faced that challenge head-on. She worked hard, learned the game inside out, and proved she was just as knowledgeable and capable as any man. With the Cardinals, Jen focused on coaching linebackers. Her role was to help these players get better at their positions. She taught them techniques and strategies. Her presence on the field changed how people saw women in football.

Katie Sowers is another groundbreaking coach. She became the first woman to coach in a Super Bowl and the first openly gay coach in the NFL. Katie's path to the NFL was full of obstacles. She played in the Women's Football Alliance for eight years, gaining valuable experience. But she faced push-back because of her gender and sexual orientation. Katie never gave up. She got a coaching internship with the Atlanta Falcons, thanks to Scott Pioli, a former NFL general manager. Later, she joined the San Francisco 49ers as part of the Bill Walsh Diversity Coaching Fellowship. As an offensive assistant, Katie's job was to help the team with their offensive strategies. She worked closely with players, helping them understand plays and improve their skills.

The contributions of these female coaches go beyond their specific roles. They have encouraged more women to pursue coaching careers. Seeing Jen and Katie on the sidelines shows girls that they can dream big and achieve those dreams. It changes how people think about women in leadership roles in football. They prove that gender doesn't determine ability. They show that hard work, knowledge, and passion are what truly matter.

Jen and Katie's success has made it easier for other women to follow in their footsteps. More teams are open to hiring female coaches. The NFL has started programs to support women in coaching roles. This increased acceptance and support are helping to change the culture of football. It's becoming more inclusive and diverse. This is good for the game because it brings in new perspectives and ideas.

Having women in coaching roles also benefits the players. Female coaches bring different experiences and viewpoints. This can help players see the game in new ways. It can also create a more supportive and understanding environment. Players learn that football is for everyone, regardless of gender. This can make them more open-minded and respectful.

THE ROLE OF WOMEN IN FOOTBALL MEDIA

When you watch a football game on TV, you might notice the reporters who bring you all the exciting updates and stories from the sidelines. Some of the most famous and respected reporters are women who have worked hard to break into this field and change the way football is covered. Erin Andrews and Pam Oliver are two of the best-known female sports journalists and broadcasters in football media. Their work has not only brought us closer to the game but also inspired many young girls to dream about a career in sports journalism.

Erin Andrews is a leading NFL sideline reporter and sportscaster. She started her career with Fox Sports Florida as a freelance reporter. She then worked with ESPN from 2004 to 2012, covering major sports events and serving as a sideline reporter for college football and basketball games. In 2012, she joined Fox Sports, becoming the lead sideline reporter for NFL broadcasts. Erin has covered some of the biggest games and moments in football, providing fans with insightful analysis and interviews. Her journey to the top was not easy. She faced challenges and had to prove herself in a field dominated by men, but her hard work and dedication paid off.

Pam Oliver has also had an extensive career covering the NFL. She has been a sideline reporter and journalist for Fox Sports for many years. Pam started her career in sports journalism after graduating from Florida A&M University. She worked at various local TV stations before joining ESPN and later Fox Sports. Pam is known for her deep knowledge of the game and her ability to connect with players and coaches. She has covered countless games and brought fans closer to the action with her insightful reports. Like Erin, Pam faced challenges and had to work hard to earn her place in football media. Her dedication and passion for the game have made her one of the most respected reporters in the field.

Both Erin Andrews and Pam Oliver have had a significant impact on football coverage. They bring a unique perspective to the game, providing analysis and stories that might otherwise go unnoticed. Their presence on the sidelines has broken down barriers and shown that women can excel in sports journalism. They have inspired other women to pursue careers in sports media, demonstrating that it is possible to succeed in a field that has traditionally been male-dominated.

Erin Andrews often shares her experiences covering high-profile NFL games. She talks about the excitement of being on the sidelines during a big game and the thrill of interviewing star players. Erin has faced challenges, such as the high-profile stalking incident that led to a legal battle, but she has remained strong and continued to excel in her career. She often speaks about the importance of perseverance and staying true to oneself. Her story is a powerful example of how hard work and determination can lead to success.

Pam Oliver has also shared her personal stories about being a woman in sports journalism. She talks about the challenges she faced early in her career and the rewards of covering the NFL. Pam has faced criticism and obstacles but has always remained focused on her love for the game and her desire to bring the best coverage to fans. She often emphasizes the importance of passion and dedication in achieving one's goals. Her journey is a testament to the impact that hard work and a deep love for the game can have on a successful career.

These women have changed the way football is covered. They have brought new insights and perspectives to the game, making it more relatable and exciting for fans. Their work has inspired many young girls to dream of careers in sports journalism and shown that with hard work and determination, anything is possible. Erin Andrews and Pam Oliver have paved the way for future generations of female sports journalists and continue to make a significant impact on the world of football.

THE GLOBALIZATION OF AMERICAN FOOTBALL: GROWING THE GAME WORLDWIDE

Imagine watching an NFL game halfway across the world, in places like London or Mexico City. Thanks to the NFL International Series, this has become a reality. These events have brought the excitement of American football to international fans, expanding the reach of the sport. London has been hosting NFL games since 2007, and each year, the games sell out quickly, filling the stadiums with enthusiastic fans. Similarly, Mexico City has hosted NFL games that draw massive crowds. By bringing these high-profile games to new audiences, the NFL is spreading a love for football far beyond the United States.

Beyond hosting games, the NFL is actively working with international football federations to promote the sport at the youth level. Programs are being developed across Europe and Asia, introducing kids to the game through training, equipment, and support. Imagine children in countries like Germany or Japan learning how to throw a football or make a tackle. These youth programs are nurturing a new generation of football players around the world, helping the sport grow from the grassroots up.

American football's popularity is steadily increasing worldwide. In Europe, leagues like the German Football League are gaining momentum, with teams from different countries competing in exciting matchups. In Asia, countries like Japan and China are also starting to embrace football, with more people tuning in to watch games and local leagues developing. As more colleges and amateur leagues pop up around the world, it's clear that football is transitioning from an American pastime to a global sport.

However, the globalization of football comes with challenges. In many countries, soccer reigns supreme, and introducing a new sport like football is no small feat. Cultural preferences and long-standing traditions make it difficult to win over fans who are deeply rooted in their own sports. Additionally, organizing international games and leagues requires significant planning and investment. Teams must travel long distances, and coordinating these events on a global scale is a logistical challenge.

Despite these hurdles, the potential for a global football community is immense. Imagine a future where football leagues exist in numerous countries, and teams from across the globe compete in international tournaments. Digital media plays a crucial role in realizing this vision, connecting fans and players worldwide. Platforms like Twitter, Instagram, and TikTok allow fans to interact with their favorite teams, share highlights, and discuss games. Streaming services make it possible to watch live games from anywhere in the world, building a sense of community among fans from different cultures and countries.

The concept of a global football league is thrilling. Imagine teams from the United States, Europe, Asia, and other regions competing in a world championship. International tournaments could showcase the best talent from around the globe, bringing fans together and elevating the sport to a new level of excitement. This would foster a worldwide celebration of football, with the best players and teams vying for global supremacy.

The future of American football is global, and we're just at the beginning of this exciting journey. As more fans, players, and countries embrace the sport, the possibilities for its growth are endless. Stay tuned for the next chapter, where we explore interactive challenges and activities to help you improve your skills and enjoy the game even more. Football's future is bright, and the world is ready to be a part of it.

———

CHAPTER 10
INTERACTIVE CHALLENGES AND ACTIVITIES

When I was a kid, my friends and I loved creating our own football challenges. We would spend hours in the backyard and the local park, setting up cones, racing against the clock, and trying to improve our skills. These moments not only made us better players but also brought us closer as friends. This chapter will help you recreate that excitement and learn new skills at home.

FOOTBALL SKILL CHALLENGES TO TRY AT HOME

Practicing football skills at home can be fun and rewarding. You don't need a big field or fancy equipment. All you need is some space, a football, and a bit of creativity. Here are some drills you can try on your own to become a better player.

A great solo drill is practicing your throwing accuracy. Find a wall and mark a few targets on it using chalk or tape. Stand a few feet away and aim to hit the targets with your throws. Start close to the wall and gradually move back as you get better. This drill improves your aim and helps you throw with precision, which is crucial for quarterbacks and other positions.

While practicing alone can be beneficial, working with a partner can enhance your skills even more. Ask a friend or family member to join you in some drills. One simple drill is passing the football back and forth. Start close together and gradually increase the distance between you. Focus on making accurate, catchable throws. This drill helps you improve your passing and catching skills while also building teamwork.

Another partner drill is practicing catching techniques. Have your partner throw the ball to you from different angles and distances. Try to catch the ball with your hands, not your body, and practice different types of catches, like over-the-shoulder and diving catches. This drill makes you a more reliable receiver and helps you react quickly to different throws.

To make your practice sessions more enjoyable, you can incorporate fun competitions. Set up a timed obstacle course that combines running and passing. For example, start by running the football through cones, then run to a target and make a throw. Time yourself and see how quickly you can complete the course. Challenge your friends or family members to see who can finish the fastest. This friendly competition not only makes practice more exciting but also pushes you to improve your skills.

Another fun competition is a catching contest. See who can catch the most passes in a row without dropping the ball. Start with easy throws and gradually make them more challenging. This contest helps you focus on catching the ball consistently and builds your confidence as a receiver.

While practicing football skills at home is fun, it's important to stay safe. Make sure you have a clear, open space for your drills. Remove any obstacles that could cause you to trip or fall. If you're practicing on grass, make sure the ground is even and free of holes. Wearing appropriate footwear is also crucial. Choose shoes that provide good support and grip to prevent slipping.

When practicing with a partner, communicate clearly and ensure both of you understand the drill. If a drill involves contact, like tackling or blocking, make sure to use proper technique to avoid injuries. Always warm up before starting your drills to prepare your muscles and prevent strains. Simple exercises like jumping jacks, leg stretches, and arm circles can help you get ready for practice.

By following these tips and trying out these drills, you'll become a better football player while having fun. Remember, practice makes perfect, and every little bit of effort helps you improve. So grab your football, find a friend or family member, and start practicing these skills today. You never know, the next football star could be you!

CREATE YOUR OWN FOOTBALL PLAYBOOK

One of the coolest things about football is the playbook. A playbook is a collection of plays that a team uses during games. It helps players know what to do on the field. In a playbook, you'll find offensive plays like passing routes and running plays. These are the plays the team uses to move the ball down the field and score points. You'll also find defensive plays like blitzes and zone coverages. These are used to stop the other team from scoring. Understanding how to create

your own playbook can make you a better player and give
you a deeper appreciation for the game.

Drawing your own playbook might sound tricky, but it's
easier than you think. Start by grabbing a piece of paper and a
pencil. To represent the players, you will use Xs and Os. The
Xs are for the defense, and the Os are for the offense. Draw a
basic football field with lines to show where each player
stands. Next, think about what you want each player to do.
For example, if you are creating a passing play, decide which
players will run routes and where the quarterback will throw
the ball. Draw lines to show the paths the players will take. If
you are designing a running play, show which players will
block and where the running back will go. Give each play a
name, like "Quick Slant" or "Power Run," so you can easily
remember and categorize them.

Being creative with your playbook is key. Think about
different situations in a game and how you would handle them.
For example, if you need to score a touchdown but only have a
few yards to go, you might design a special goal-line play. This
play could involve a quick pass or a powerful run straight up the
middle. Trick plays are another fun way to get creative. These are
plays that trick the defense into thinking you are doing one thing
when you are actually doing something else. One famous trick

play is the "Flea Flicker." In this play, the quarterback hands the ball to the running back, who runs a few steps and then throws the ball back to the quarterback. The quarterback then throws a long pass to a receiver downfield. Trick plays can be risky, but when they work, they are exciting and can change the game.

To help inspire you, let's look at a few famous plays. The "Hail Mary" pass is a last-second play where the quarterback throws the ball as far as he can toward the end zone. This play is often used when the team needs a touchdown and there's not much time left on the clock. The goal is for one of the receivers to catch the ball and score. Another famous play is the "Flea Flicker," which we mentioned earlier. This play uses misdirection to catch the defense off guard. Another fun play is the "Statue of Liberty." In this play, the quarterback pretends to throw a pass but secretly hands the ball to a running back behind his back. The running back then runs the ball, surprising the defense.

Creating a playbook allows you to think like a coach and understand the strategy behind the game. It helps you see the bigger picture and makes you a smarter player. Plus, it's a lot of fun to come up with your own plays and see if they work. So grab some paper, get creative, and start designing your own football playbook. You never know, one of your plays might just be the next big thing in football!

QUIZZES TO TEST YOUR FOOTBALL KNOWLEDGE

Quizzes can be a fun way to see how much you know about football. They can help you learn new things and test your memory. Let's start with some multiple-choice questions. These questions will cover different parts of the game. For example, do you know which team has won the most Super Bowls (hint: we already told you)? Here are your options: (A) New England Patriots, (B) Pittsburgh Steelers, (C) Dallas Cowboys, or (D) San Francisco 49ers. Think carefully before you choose. The correct answer is Pittsburgh Steelers and New England Patriots, each with six Super Bowl wins. Isn't that cool?

Next, let's try a true or false question. True or False: The quarterback is responsible for calling the plays. If you said "True," you're right! The quarterback often tells the team what play they will run next. This is one of the most important jobs on the field. The quarterback has to know all the plays and make quick decisions.

Now, let's move on to some questions about the rules of football. How many points is a touchdown worth? This one might be easy if you watch football games often. A touchdown is worth six points. Teams can score extra points after a touchdown by kicking the ball through the goalposts for one point or trying to run or pass the ball into the end zone again for two points.

What about football history? Who was the first player to rush for 2,000 yards in a season? Here are your options: (A) O.J. Simpson, (B) Barry Sanders, (C) Eric Dickerson, or (D) Emmitt Smith. The answer is O.J. Simpson. He set this record in 1973, and it was a big deal because no one had done it before.

Let's mix in some fun and challenging questions. Some questions are easier, like "What color is the penalty flag used by referees?" If you said yellow, you're correct! Referees throw yellow flags to show that a penalty has happened. These flags help everyone know when the rules have been broken.

Now for a more challenging question: "Which player

holds the record for the most career sacks?" This one might be a bit tougher. The answer is Bruce Smith. He has 200 career sacks, which is an incredible achievement. Sacking the quarterback means tackling him behind the line of scrimmage, stopping the play. It's a big deal for defensive players.

To make these quizzes even more interesting, let's include explanations and fun facts for each answer. For example, why is a touchdown worth six points? The scoring system in football was designed to balance the difficulty of scoring with the reward. A touchdown is worth more points because it is harder to achieve than a field goal or an extra point.

Here's another fun fact: Do you know why the term "Hail Mary" is used for long, desperate passes? The term became famous after a game in 1975 when Dallas Cowboys quarterback Roger Staubach threw a last-second, long pass to win the game. After the game, Staubach said he closed his eyes and said a "Hail Mary" prayer before throwing the ball. The name stuck, and now it's used to describe any long, last-ditch effort to score.

Quizzes are a great way to learn while having fun. They can help you remember important facts and understand the game better. Plus, you can challenge your friends and family to see who knows the most about football. So grab a piece of paper and a pencil, or just use your memory, and try to answer come up with more questions for future games with your friends!

————

AFTERWORD

When I set out to write this book, I had a simple goal. I wanted to share my passion for football with young readers like you. I aim to make football more accessible and exciting. I hope you are inspired by the stories of legendary players, and that you learned the basics of the rules and strategies of the game. I hope you see how football can teach valuable life lessons, like perseverance and teamwork.

Throughout this book, we've taken an exciting journey together. We started by exploring the origins and evolution of football. We learned how American football grew from simple European games. We saw how key figures like Walter Camp shaped the sport. We discovered important milestones, like the founding of the NFL and the rise of college football.

Then, we dived deep into the stories of legendary players. We learned about Walter Payton's hard work and kindness. We saw how Peyton Manning's intelligence and preparation made him a great quarterback. We marveled at Tom Brady's journey from an overlooked player to a record-breaking legend. We also explored the inspirational stories of players like Jim Thorpe, Jerry Rice, Bo Jackson, Lawrence Taylor, and Patrick Mahomes.

In the next chapters, we broke down the game itself. We explained the basic rules of football, from scoring points to understanding penalties. We looked at offensive and defensive formations and the critical role of the quarterback. We also explored special teams and the importance of game film and analysis.

We moved on to skills and drills. We learned how to improve passing accuracy, master tackling, and increase speed and agility. We saw exercises for wide receivers and linemen. These drills will help you become a better player on the field.

We also relived some of football's iconic games and unforgettable moments. We felt the excitement of the "Immaculate Reception" and the drama of the "Miracle at the Meadowlands." We saw how football moments create lasting memories.

In our culture chapter, we shared the joy of tailgating and learned about famous football stadiums. We saw how football impacts American society, from Thanksgiving games to the Super Bowl. We explored the passion of football fans and their unique traditions.

We didn't stop there. We looked at inspirational stories of perseverance. We learned from Rudy Ruettiger's journey and Kurt Warner's rise from grocery store shelves to Super Bowl glory. We saw how Alex Smith's comeback showed incredible resilience. We also shared stories of young players who overcame challenges.

We had fun with football trivia and facts. We tested our

knowledge and learned new things. We discovered record-breaking moments and famous quotes. We even looked at some bizarre football moments that made us laugh and wonder.

Finally, we peeked into the future of football. We saw the rise of women's football leagues and the impact of female coaches and journalists. We explored how technology is changing training and gameplay. We imagined a world where football is a truly global sport.

What are the key takeaways from this book? Football is more than just a game. It's a journey filled with lessons and excitement. It teaches us hard work, perseverance, and team-work. It connects us with friends, family, and fans. It creates unforgettable moments and memories. It continues to evolve and inspire.

I encourage you to take what you've learned and put it into practice. Grab a football and try out the drills. Create your own playbook and imagine new strategies. Test your knowledge with trivia questions. Share the stories and facts with your friends. Keep exploring the world of football. There is always something new to learn and discover.

Now, here's my call to action for you. Don't just be a reader. Be a player, a fan, a coach, and a learner. Embrace the spirit of football. Get out there and play. Enjoy the game, cheer for your team, and share your love for football with others. Remember, every great player started as a learner just like you. Your journey is just beginning.

Thank you for joining me on this journey through the world of football. I hope this book has inspired and excited you. I hope it has given you the knowledge and confidence to dive deeper into the game. Most of all, I hope it has shown you the joy and magic of football. Keep chasing your dreams, both on and off the field. The future of football is bright, and you are a part of it.

Keep playing, keep learning, and keep dreaming. The game is yours.

———

If you enjoyed this book, please consider leaving a review.

GLOSSARY

AFC Championship: A championship game in the American Football Conference (AFC), which will determine the AFC's representative at the Super Bowl.

Backfield: The area located behind the line of scrimmage and where each play will begin once the ball is snapped.

Blitz: When the defense sends a higher number of defenders (typically, five or more) to charge the quarterback.

Block: To obstruct defensive players from tackling the ball carrier or sacking the quarterback.

Complete: A successful forward pass from the quarterback that is caught by a receiver.

Down: One of four consecutive attempts for the offense to move the ball at least 10 yards forward.

End zone: Between the goal line and the end line at each end of the field, this is the area where touchdowns are scored.

Field Goal: When a kicker kicks the football in between the football goalposts and above the crossbar for three points.

Gridiron: An alternative to describe an American football field and another name for the sport itself.

Incomplete interception: When a defensive player catches a pass that was intended for an offensive receiver, leading to a turnover.

Line of scrimmage: An imaginary line that stretches the width of the field where the football is placed at the start of a down and on either side of which the offense and defense line up. No player can cross this line before the ball is snapped.

Move the chains: A colloquialism that means the offense is making progress; when the offense achieves a first down, the signal poles on the sidelines (which are essentially 2 tall sticks with a chain connecting them) are moved to the new measurement spot for the next set of four downs.

NFC Championship: A championship game in the National Football Conference (NFC), which will determine the NFC's representative at the Super Bowl.

Overtime: Play that occurs after regular time if the scores are deadlocked after the fourth quarter.

Play: A move or strategic maneuver in a game.

Playoffs: The postseason tournament in which the top teams from each conference compete for the championship title.

Point after: One point is given to a team after their kicker successfully kicks the football between the goalposts and above the crossbar, following a touchdown.

Rush: To gain yardage by running forward with the football.

Sack: A tackle on a quarterback while he possesses the football behind the line of scrimmage.

Scrimmage: The clash of opposing linemen at every down.

Shotgun: When the quarterback lines up for a snap relatively far behind the line of scrimmage.

Snap: When the center passes the ball back from the line of scrimmage to the quarterback and signals the start of each play.

Special Team: Various positions in a football team that are deployed in various game situations, such as kickoffs and attempts at field goals, where the standard offensive and defensive formations are not appropriate.

Super Bowl: The final championship game where the AFC champion will play the NFC champion for the title of the best football team of the season.

Touchdown: The act of catching or running the football in an opponent's end zone.

Wild card games: Playoff games featuring NFL teams that didn't win their respective divisions but still qualified for the postseason due to their impressive regular-season performances.

BIBLIOGRAPHY

American football. (n.d.). In *Wikipedia*. https://en.wikipedia.org/wiki/American_football

Burch, C. (2020, February 3). Meet the American who shaped modern football: Walter Camp, pigskin pioneer. *Fox News*. https://www.foxnews.com/lifestyle/meet-american-shaped-modern-football-walter-camp-pigskin-pioneer

McCarthy, M. (2018, September 17). The birth of the National Football League. *History*. https://www.history.com/news/the-birth-of-the-national-football-league

Draft Countdown. (n.d.). The role of college football in American sports culture. https://www.draftcountdown.com/other/the-role-of-college-football-in-american-sports-culture/

Walter Payton. (n.d.). In *Encyclopaedia Britannica*. https://www.britannica.com/biography/Walter-Payton

Peyton Manning. (n.d.). In *Wikipedia*. https://en.wikipedia.org/wiki/Peyton_Manning

Tom Brady. (n.d.). In *Encyclopaedia Britannica*. https://www.britannica.com/biography/Tom-Brady

Roffman, M. (2020, July 1). How Jim Thorpe became America's first multi-sport star. *History*. https://www.history.com/news/jim-thorpe-sports-native-american-athlete-olympics

Football. (n.d.). In *Britannica Kids*. https://kids.britannica.com/kids/article/football/353142

NFL Operations. (n.d.). Formations 101. https://operations.nfl.com/learn-the-game/nfl-basics/formations-101/

25 greatest quarterbacks in NFL history. (2016, August 29). *Athlon Sports*. https://athlonsports.com/nfl/25-greatest-quarterbacks-nfl-history-2016

Gola, R. (2023, September 5). The importance of special teams in football. *Lafayette Ledger*. https://lafayetteledger.org/29548/sports/the-importance-of-special-teams-in-football/

Youth Football Online. (n.d.). Quarterback passing drills and techniques | QB drills. https://youthfootballonline.com/drillsquarterback/

Youth Football Online. (n.d.). How to tackle with proper tackling technique.

https://youthfootballonline.com/how-to-tackle-with-proper-tackling-tech
nique-in-youth-football/

Glen Burnie Fitness and Nutrition. (n.d.). Speed and agility training for teens and kids. https://glenburniefitnessandnutrition.com/speed-and-agility-training-for-teens-and-kids/

Competitive Drive Training. (2018, June 13). Wide receiver 101 part III: Catching. https://competitivedrivetraining.wordpress.com/2018/06/13/wide-receiver-101-part-iii-catching/

The Immaculate Reception: Catch of a lifetime. (n.d.). *Pro Football Hall of Fame.* https://www.profootballhof.com/football-history/the-immaculate-recep tion-catch-of-a-lifetime/

Casserly, P. (2018, November 14). Miracle at the Meadowlands: The fumble that changed everything. *Sports Illustrated.* https://www.si.com/nfl/2018/11/14/miracle-meadowlands-40th-anniversary-giants-eagles-joe-pisarcik-herman-edwards-harry-carson

Super Bowl XLII. (n.d.). In *Wikipedia.* https://en.wikipedia.org/wiki/Super_Bowl_XLII

O'Hare, M. (2020, January 8). The Music City Miracle: An oral history of one of NFL's most memorable moments. *Tennessean.* https://www.tennessean.com/story/sports/nfl/titans/2020/01/08/music-city-miracle-oral-history-titans-bills-anniversary/2798498001/

Tailgating: The history. (n.d.). *American Heritage.* https://www.americanher itage.com/tailgating-history

Mark, J. (2011, January 3). The 10 most storied landmarks in NFL history. *Bleacher Report.* https://bleacherreport.com/articles/625484-the-10-most-storied-landmarks-in-nfl-history

Draft Countdown. (n.d.). Exploring the impact of American football on society. https://www.draftcountdown.com/other/beyond-the-game-exploring-the-impact-of-american-football-on-society/

BestColleges. (n.d.). The 10 best college football traditions. https://www.best colleges.com/news/analysis/10-best-college-football-traditions/

Hutton, C. (2020, January 10). Rudy Ruettiger: The true story of the Notre Dame walk-on. *All That's Interesting.* https://allthatsinteresting.com/rudy-ruettiger

Leahy, P. (2011, November 22). Kurt Warner's grocery-store checker to NFL MVP story: A tale of perseverance. *Bleacher Report.* https://bleacherreport.com/articles/1190204-kurt-warners-grocery-store-checker-to-nfl-mvp-story-a-tale-of-perseverance

Reutter, C. (2020, July 30). Alex Smith's comeback: Inside the fight to save the

QB's leg and life. *ESPN.* https://www.espn.com/nfl/story/_/id/29112995/alex-smith-comeback-fight-save-qb-leg-life

Wilborn, T. (2013, October 21). Peyton Manning on his neck surgeries rehab—and how he almost didn't make it back. *The Washington Post.* https://www.washingtonpost.com/sports/redskins/peyton-manning-on-his-neck-surgeries-rehab--and-how-he-almost-didnt-make-it-back/2013/10/21/8e3b5ca6-3a55-11e3-b7ba-503fb5822c3e_story.html

290 NFL historical trivia questions, answers, and fun facts. (n.d.). *Fun Trivia.* https://www.funtrivia.com/en/Sports/NFL-Historical-661.html

32 teams: Fun fact on every NFL football team. (n.d.). *107.5 The Fan.* https://1075thefan.com/playlist/32-teams-fun-fact-on-every-nfl-football-team/

10 record-breaking moments in football history every student fan should know. (2020, October 7). *Ultra Tifo.* https://www.ultras-tifo.net/news/7626-10-record-breaking-moments-in-football-history-every-student-fan-should-know.html

Antoniacci, M. (2021, January 24). 28 of the greatest quotes from NFL legends. *Inc.* https://www.inc.com/mandy-antoniacci/28-of-the-greatest-quotes-from-nfl-legends.html

Women's Football Alliance. (n.d.). Professional women's tackle football. https://wfaprofootball.com/

Gross, E. (2020, February 1). Katie Sowers will make history as the first woman to coach at the Super Bowl. *Forbes.* https://www.forbes.com/sites/elanagross/2020/02/01/katie-sowers-will-make-history-as-the-first-woman-to-coach-at-the-super-bowl/

Erin Andrews. (n.d.). In *Wikipedia.* https://en.wikipedia.org/wiki/Erin_Andrews

Higher Echelon. (n.d.). How the NFL leverages virtual reality sports training. https://www.higherechelon.com/how-the-nfl-leverages-virtual-reality-sports-training/

Top 5 at-home football drills. (n.d.). *Football Tutorials.* https://www.football-tutorials.com/at-home-football-drills/

The five best trick plays in football. (n.d.). *Electro-Mech.* https://www.electro-mech.com/team-sports/football/the-five-best-trick-plays-in-football/

90 American football for kids trivia questions, answers, and fun facts. (n.d.). *Fun Trivia.* https://www.funtrivia.com/en/ForChildren/American-Football-for-Kids-18001.html

Football plays 101: How to design a killer playbook. (n.d.). *Football Tutorials.* https://www.football-tutorials.com/football-plays-101/

IMAGE REFERENCES

Alchetron. (n.d.). *Music city miracle.* Retrieved October 6, 2024, from https://
    alchetron.com/cdn/music-city-miracle-ef1a6adb-a8c9-43ec-8fed-
    9be5f7d8cf3-resize-750.jpeg

Curiel, A. (2017). *NFL wall* [Image]. Unsplash. https://unsplash.com/photos/
    nfl-logo-KgYazRO3l8A

Goldsberry, P. (2019). *Fans watching football at home* [Image]. Unsplash. https://
    unsplash.com/photos/person-in-blue-nba-dallas-mavericks-crew-neck-
    shirt-sitting-while-holding-bowl-with-potato-chips-Ldl5WoUQmBk

Johnston, K. (2017b). *Football players battle for position in a college football game*
    [Image].   Unsplash.   https://unsplash.com/photos/two-nfl-players-
    ym7zKXHdCSY

Johnston, K. (2019). Football catch [Image]. Pixabay. https://pixabay.com/
    photos/football-american-football-player-1490180/

Johnstone, K. (2017). *A college football player prepares to begin a game with a kick-
    off.* [Image]. Unsplash. https://unsplash.com/photos/three-football-play
    ers-running-towards-football-ball-at-field-during-daytime-ZH66-9B04cw

Keithjj. (2022a). *Football tackle* [Image]. Pixabay. https://pixabay.com/photos/
    football-american-football-ball-1518040/

Keithjj. (2024a). *American football fan with face painted* [Image]. Pixabay. https://
    pixabay.com/photos/american-football-fan-supporter-1505842/

Keithjj. (2024c). *Quarterback throwing a forward pass* [Image]. Pixabay. https://
    pixabay.com/photos/football-american-football-players-1485698/

Li, Z. (2024). *Football field* [Image]. Pixabay. https://www.pexels.com/photo/
    healthy-light-city-field-13811359/

Library of Congress. (2019). *Early days of American Football* [Image]. Unsplash.
    https://unsplash.com/photos/football-players-red-grange-and-joe-zeller-
    during-practice-nJD0PWqDOBw

mauricioglucas. (2024). *Barbecue in the street* [Image]. Pixabay. https://pixabay.
    com/photos/barbecue-in-the-street-beef-barbecue-4281088/

NFL. (n.d.). *Pittsburgh Steelers image.* Retrieved October 6, 2024, from https://
    static.clubs.nfl.com/image/private/t_editorial_landscape_12_desktop/
    steelers/k1umkxj25ojgtm9qrpyx

Pinterest. (n.d.). *Football image.* Retrieved October 6, 2024, from https://i.
    pinimg.com/originals/ef/6a/56/ef6a5695306dcbd5b9fbc7b4f5c79b41.jpg

Pixabay. (2023). *Football center getting ready to snap the ball* [Image]. Pexels.
    https://www.pexels.com/photo/football-player-game-position-163398/

Sports Illustrated. (n.d.). *The fumble that changed football.* Retrieved October 6,

2024,   from   https://www.si.com/.image/t_share/MTY4MDMwNDg0N
TY3MDQxNDA4/the-fumble-chnaged-football-01jpg.jpg

Unsplash+. (2022). *Timeout* [Image]. Unsplash. https://unsplash.com/photos/
a-group-of-football-players-kneel-down-on-the-field-NvANG2wuKPo

Verduzco, M. (2023). *Playbook on a football field* [Image]. Unsplash. https://
unsplash.com/photos/a-notebook-sitting-on-the-side-of-a-football-field-
Rn6n5Lh1BdA

Williams, J. (2021). *American football* [Image]. Unsplash. https://unsplash.
com/photos/a-close-up-of-a-football-on-a